Parenting Boys

The Complete Guide to Being a Parent

(Essential Tips for New Mums a Guide to the First Weeks of Motherhood)

Roger Ruben

Published by Rob Miles

© **Roger Ruben**

All Rights Reserved

Parenting Boys: The Complete Guide to Being a Parent (Essential Tips for New Mums a Guide to the First Weeks of Motherhood)

ISBN 9781990084409

All rights reserved. No part of this guide may be reproduced in any form without permission in writing from the publisher except in the case of brief quotations embodied in critical articles or reviews.

Legal & Disclaimer

The information contained in this book is not designed to replace or take the place of any form of medicine or professional medical advice. The information in this book has been provided for educational and entertainment purposes only.

The information contained in this book has been compiled from sources deemed reliable, and it is accurate to the best of the Author's knowledge; however, the Author cannot guarantee its accuracy and validity and cannot be held liable for any errors or omissions. Changes are periodically made to this book. You must consult your doctor or get professional medical advice before using any of the suggested remedies, techniques, or information in this book.

Upon using the information contained in this book, you agree to hold harmless the Author from and against any damages, costs, and expenses, including any legal fees potentially resulting from the application of any of the information provided by this guide. This disclaimer applies to any damages or injury caused by the use and application, whether directly or indirectly, of any advice or information presented, whether for breach of contract, tort, negligence, personal injury, criminal intent, or under any other cause of action.

You agree to accept all risks of using the information presented inside this book. You need to consult a professional medical practitioner in order to ensure you are both able and healthy enough to participate in this program.

Table of Contents

INTRODUCTION 1

CHAPTER 1: DEVELOPING AND CLARIFYING CLEAR COMMUNICATIVE EXPECTATIONS 4

CHAPTER 2: CONNECTING WITH YOUR CHILD REQUIRES TWO-WAY COMMUNICATION 13

CHAPTER 3: SEE THINGS FROM THEIR PERSPECTIVE 16

CHAPTER 4: MODELS OF PARENTING DURING DIVORCE .. 21

CHAPTER 5: HOW PARENTS' INVOLVEMENT AFFECTS THEIR KIDS 29

CHAPTER 6: SECRET TO BEING A GREAT STEP DAD 34

CHAPTER 7: TWO ESSENTIAL PARENTING TRAITS 39

CHAPTER 8: WHAT IS DEPRESSION? 48

CHAPTER 9: HOW TO CHOOSE THE RIGHT DISCIPLINE METHOD 52

CHAPTER 10: HOW DO PARENTS COMMUNICATE EFFECTIVELY WITH A TODDLER? 59

CHAPTER 11: AGGRESSIVE BEHAVIOUR 66

CHAPTER 12: POTTY TRAINING 71

CHAPTER 13: TODDLER TANTRUM AND HISSY FIT SOLUTIONS 77

CHAPTER 14: COMMUNICATION IS CRUCIAL FOR DIVORCED COUPLES WITH CHILDREN 92

CHAPTER 15: FAMILY ACTIVITIES YOU CAN DO OUTDOORS FOR EXERCISE 99

CHAPTER 16: LET KIDS BE THEMSELVES 103

CHAPTER 17: TIPS FOR BUILDING SELF ESTEEM 112

CHAPTER 18: CHORES WITH CHILDREN 120

CHAPTER 19: SECURITY 126

CHAPTER 20: HELPING YOUR CHILD OVERCOME FEAR AND BECOME COURAGEOUS 134

CHAPTER 21: NO TWO KIDS ARE THE SAME 145

CHAPTER 22: STRATEGIC LISTENING 148

CHAPTER 23: TRANSITION STRATEGIES 152

CHAPTER 24: SUMMARY AND TIPS 159

CHAPTER 25: EDUCATION WOES 164

CHAPTER 26: WHEN ROYALS PRODUCE PEASANTS 168

CHAPTER 27: HOW AND WHEN TO INTRODUCE A NEW RELATIONSHIP 176

CONCLUSION 181

Introduction

In life today, society sees more and more single parents being left to bring up children. Since the natural assumption of people is that a child has two parents, it can be very difficult for the single dad to raise his kids without feeling some guilt and feeling also that they have something to explain about the reason they are tackling the upbringing of the kids on their own. People expect a woman to do this job. They expect mothering instincts to kick in when divorce happens, but often the father is the better choice for the children and can make a wonderful job of parenting alone once they get past all the barriers that seem to get in the way.

This book looks at single parenting from the male perspective for a purpose. While it is understandable that a woman may find herself looking after kids, men are taking on this role because of necessity and are becoming extremely good at it, but because of society pressures, are forced to explain their circumstances over and over again, reliving the anger and the negativity of what brought them to this situation in the first place. No real explanation is needed once a father understands that it's now that counts. The children need him and there is certainly no need to bring the anger of the old relationship into the picture.

The other feeling that a man may experience is a feeling of guilt. Often men have to go out to earn a living and may feel that they are less accessible to children when the children need them. This leads to a lot of guilty feelings in all directions. Taking time off work to deal with a parenting problem may cause difficulty at work, but it's almost like the man is being torn between two worlds. This book gives answers on how to deal with these problems that may lie ahead and help parents to avoid bitterness and anger that bring with them so much negativity.

My dad was a joy to me, and this dedication he had to our childhood was a credit to him. He carried guilt and excuses for many years before he realized that we, his kids, didn't need him to apologize and that we loved him for who he was, regardless of whether he was still with our mother or not. This is written to help those fathers who, like my father, don't understand the situation from the child's perspective.

Chapter 1: Developing And Clarifying Clear Communicative Expectations

misconduct, there In order to discipline a child for must be a game plan or a strategy to train them as to how to behave (Sanders, 1999). Also, if parents desire their children to be successful in their conduct, they must model their behavior properly however this will be addressed later.

First, there must be clear basis for the expectation of both parents for what they want & the rudiments to parenting. Parents, depending upon what is deemed as good and bad, or on the background, within reason, must communicate & plan their expectation to each other. They may simply start by making up an expectations list (such as family oriented, academic, religious, social, hygiene or personal experience) for various activities & settings so as to be very concrete & specific in teaching the children. Some expectations are more compelling than others; however, child's ability, age, resources & growth status that are available to the family must be taken into consideration by parents. For instance, the expectation from a four year old tyke to get ready family supper and after that rebuffing him for not meeting the desires is extremely nonsensical because of his formative status and age, as should be obvious. In a book named Common Sense Parenting, Burke maintains that the following three queries must be accounted for while checking whether the desires are sensible: 1) that whether you have educated the expectation to your tykes, 2) Are they able to fully comprehend the expectation given, & 3) Are they capable of presenting & performance (Burke, 1987). It's obvious the three aforementioned queries cover the larger part of whether the expectations are suited to their child or not based on his age and capacity. Second, Once appropriate rules & expectations are set for the child, the following step is the communication of those set of rules to their child whether in deed or through word. Another thing to remember is how one plans to verbally pass on those expectations. The other thing to remember is how one is going to endorse those expectations through conduct & behavior. The child will be able to catch more from what parents act out to him or her.

Another effective way of imparting those expectations is through arranging a family get-together. The family can plan out which set of rules are preferable along with any clarifications or interests going on between both children and parents to be held. This will only increase the behavior for Tykes for the best wishes to give and push can bring confusion, anger and resentment in the Tyke (Dinkmeyer and McKay, 1989).

Staying calm is an important application of positive or negative for the behavior of his son consequences element. If Ray Burke says "children can be sarcastic, rebel, rebel, and perhaps violence. Parents should prepare for such moments and learn to stay calm. Sometimes, parents get so offensive on the conduct of their children that they are incapable of thinking properly. Parents must know their bounds when the tyke grows, they must know what is going around them, and deflect back circumstances made up to respond correctly otherwise. In a book named as "Common Sense Parenting", Burke suggests: rehearse constructive considering, not what the kid says by and by, to keep the emphasis on practices as opposed to what is accepted to be the purposes behind the awful conduct of his child, and in the event that he ever gets irate and say or accomplish something that you lament, dependably backpedal and say you apologize.

1. Consequences and Consistency

Positive results lead to energize or aggrandize attractive attitude. The right instance of when to implement positive follow-up is to catch your child obeying directions & manifesting good behavior. The rewards emerging from positive consequences range from short term rewards (extra playtime or sweets) to long term rewards (outings, gifts etc). Additionally you should utilize positive results that will suit your tyke, and utilizing outcomes that don't cost much. Reward incentive planning helps forming children conducts (Dodson, 1988). A rundown of activities you need him to do less of, encouraging him when the chance to resist is given however maintained a strategic distance from, and a rundown of activities you need him to accomplish a greater amount of (Dodson, 1988). The explanation made above gives fairly clear view why and when positive consequences come into play

The negative outcomes are characterized as "injecting a negative outcome to lessen or avoid certain practices, which are inappropriate, or depriving the tyke of what he holds dear is costly". Absence of TV in the house and spending additional time on doing chores are instances of negative consequences. Children happen to espouse a strategy to avoid such negative consequences. Burke maintains, "It's quite challenging to find a negative consequence that works adequately and remember to stay serene when your child misbehaves (Burke, Pardini, and Loeber, 2008). Calmness and serenity upon misbehavior helps affect your child learn the right behavior.

Anything he says absolutely retains no validity and breaks up to failure if it does not occur consistently. "Consistency is the backbone of discipline". If Cutts says in his book, "Better Home Discipline" that there must be bend ability in what you forebears from, asks and in what you execute... if not, the disparity between the two parents can lead to a series of panic (Cutts, 1952) "for a child, inconsistency contains double messages. Children need to ensure their position in what they stand. "Consistency is the key to being a good parent, the child who was reliable and serious".

2. "Being a Role Model to Your Child"

"Do what I say and not what I do" is a phrase that is repeated very often; however children are the only focus of it. Children aren't going to-do what parent says, because they'll do what model parents present to them. "Children model the behaviors that the parent may have presented to them again and again". Exhibiting messages before a child can be easily seen by analyzing their behavior. The main objective is that parents always put a positive example according to which children can be modeled (Burke, 1997).

RPG correct behavior with children is a different model of behavior. It's easier to teach your child a right conduct by role playing than through punishments. In any situation practicing the right thing increase the chances of success. "Robert Eimers" provides a format for role in four easy steps to help parents teach their children proper behavior. These four points are: 1)Assuming roles and exchanging them with the child, 2), set the stage, acting out the situation caused by the child; 3) start the role-play, and 4) be sarcastic on necessary occasions over performance, with honors, if necessary (Eimers and Aitchison, 1977). A child can helped by techniques such as role-playing to think ahead and repeat to adapt situations that could be frustrating.

3. Effective Praising

In Lopez, (2004), Ray Burke says, "Praise is powerful. Admiration of your child is one of the most important things you can do as a parent. Praise is a food for growth – an appreciation. It nourishes your child emotionally, as a food helps your child grow physically" (Lopez, 2004)).There can be no better summing up of the of praise effects than this. Praise is a way focusing on the positive aspects in every situation. Charles Schaefers book "How to Influence Children", says the praise is to give a "positive and realistic assessment of the performance of a child".

One of the perks of praise is to boost up child's self-esteem, to develop a belief in them, in addition to feel secure within one self. There is a sense of self-belief when one is aware is aware someone has encouraged them by paying attention to with positive attitude, due to their efforts. Praise, says Norma Cutts, proliferates one's "well-being" (Cutts, 1952). Therefore, it would encourage your child's passion to perform whatever task they are given with "if you help them out with appraisal & remarks of admiration.

Chapter 2: Connecting With Your Child Requires Two-Way Communication

As parents one of the most difficult challenges we have is effectively communicating with our kids. We have tried many times to establish two-way communication with them but it seems they are not quite as interested as we are to participate in the conversation. Their attention span is very limited and we find ourselves asking many questions to receive a response. Wait a minute here, who does this sound like? Just this morning while we were busy reading the paper; they were the ones asking the questions when our attention was focused on the latest headlines. Then there was last night when we were working on the computer? No wonder everyone is frustrated with all the lack of attention going on.

If you haven't noticed our kids are distracted very easily and getting any kind of response from them is difficult when they are in their own world. As parents we are responsible to demonstrate the correct patterns of communication. In turn they must learn correct two-way communication and it is not acceptable to ignore it. We must early on educate them what are the proper ways to communicate to prevent any non-verbal agreements from taking hold. There should be total focus on them and what is being discussed. Let them learn by your example.

Continue educating them by talking and explaining to them using age-appropriate terms why their way of communicating doesn't work. Show your kids how to effectively communicate even though it may be hard for them to understand. Do not stop until all of their questions are answered.

Just as we are asking them to listen so must we be active listeners. Listen to their side of the story or opinions and make sure you understand where they are coming from.

As parents we must be consistent and send the same message each time we talk with our kids. Let them know that whenever their two-way communication is lacking in effort on their part you will make them aware of it with the opportunity to get back on track.

Although connecting with your child requires two-way communication there will be times when they lack focus and will not communicate. As the expert we are the best judge on how much improvement they are making in their communications. Being the role model with positive communication patterns is the best way to ensure they continue expanding their two-way communication skills.

Chapter 3: See Things From Their Perspective

Most often, parents have the misconception that they know everything about their children.They often think that their children would follow what they say especially if they insisted to them to do what they want.

They seem to forget how is it to be young, especially on an adolescent stage where rebelliousness seemed to be the only way out.They always insist on their own way knowing that their children will follow them or else, there would always be equivalent punishments.However, without their knowledge, their children may have already been silently grudging everything that they impose to them.

Not knowing how their treatments have caused so much damage, until such time that they could no longer control their children.Thus, becoming an effective parent, it is best to note that there are some things in life that their children need to be heard for. The following are some of the ways on how parents could actually get through the barriers that their children have been putting up against them. Through knowing their children's perspectives, a happier life with them could and CAN be readily achieved.

Reflective Listening

In terms of psychology, adolescence is the transitional stage of the teenagers wherein they tend to be more confused with their lives as they begin to experience physiological changes in their bodies. This stage is most difficult for them especially if their views and opinions are criticized, mocked, or not heeded.

Most teenagers have been known to act on impulse based on their true feelings and without giving much thought to the possible consequences of their actions. Parents should understand this stage more than anyone else since they too have passed through similar situations before.They are the ones who could always help their children understand certain views and become allies rather than critics. Parents need to know more their kids through reflective listening, not just plainly listening to their qualms but understanding how the kids' perspectives are in order to understand them completely.It has always been known that parents only hear the words their children have spoken but never ever tried understanding the real meaning behind those words.If they never like what their children said they always tend to be more critical rather than consoling.Parents should always give time to reflect the words their children have spoken through keen listening to the meanings behind their words.It would be quite difficult to do so since they still have so many things to do in their lives but by becoming more understanding could make some difference to the lives of their children.

Empathizing

Putting oneself in the shoes of the other, this has always been known as empathy.Parents should always learn the art of empathizing especially with their children in order to understand their perspectives.Parents must always understand that teenagers never have the patience to explain further how they feel.Words such as, "nothing", "you never want to know", or "you understand a bit" are often heard from teenagers who are estranged to their parents.Once parents hear these from their children they need to be alarmed and do something to alleviate the situation.If parents would continue to insist their ways, the more that their children would never open up to them.The best thing for parents to do in this situation is to become more empathic.By constantly making themselves available for their children and be more supportive could strengthen the bond between them.However, it could always take time for the children to open up, but parents need to be more patient and accept the decision of their children as well.

Chapter 4: Models Of Parenting During Divorce

Since there are such a large number of families experiencing divorce, there has been and continues to be a huge amount of research completed on the topic every year. Professionals that work with families in divorce (including Child Development Specialists, Consultants, Family Therapists, Play Therapists, Psychologist and Psychiatrists) all conduct routine evaluations of how different types of parenting styles or models impact on children. This research indicates that there are basically three models used by parents in most areas, although they may be known by different names in different countries. For purposes of this discussion these parenting models will be known as:

- ☐ Independet Parenting
- ☐ Parallel Parenting
- ☐ CeParenting

The models are discussed from the most distant type of model to the highest level of communication, collaboration and dual parent interaction with regards to the children. Parents may find that in the initial phases of the divorce when the emotional level is high, the first two may be more practical and manageable, but parents should be working towards the third model, the collaborative co-parenting model as the ultimate parenting through divorce goal.

INDEPENDENT PARENTING

Independent parenting is really exactly what you may expect the term to mean. In this parenting arrangement each parent manages their own rules, expectations and day-to-day routines with respect to the children when the children are in their care. To avoid confusion, having custody of the children will be known as parenting time in this book. So, in independent parenting models, when it is Mom's parenting time she makes the rules, sets discipline and handles all issues without consultation with Dad. Dad likewise sets rules, develops discipline policies and handless the decisions when the kids are with him, again without consultation with Mom.

Most parents, especially those with older children, can quickly see that this can be a potential disaster in the making. The problems with independent parenting models are:

- ☐ Kids quickly learn Mom and Dad are not talking or collaborating, and may take advantage of the situation by play both parents off each other. In the worse case scenario these kids will be literally living two lives disconnected from each other without the ability to talk about or comment on what is happening in their other home.

- ☐ All children need structure and predictability in their life. This model may not provide any structure or predictability, especially if Mom and Dad have very different views of parenting. Kids may be highly confused if rules, expectations and discipline are vastly different between homes.

- Kids don't have the opportunity to continue to see and understand both parents are working together; rather they clearly see that Mom and Dad are in conflict and not interacting. This may teach children all the wrong skills needed to be effective communicators and problem solvers in their own lives.

In very high conflict situations independent parenting may be first step or model that most parents use. Working with a family therapist, communication or conflict coach, parenting co-ordinator or other professional can help parents get back on track with communication and positive and productive interactions with regards to the children.

PARALLEL PARENTING

Parallel parenting is still a limited interaction model between the two parents, and is the one most often used by parents in the period directly after the divorce. In parallel parenting both parents work together to achieve the same goals for their children.

A great way to picture this is to think of a railroad track. Each parent is one rail of the track, both heading in the same direction to make sure the train (or child in this case) gets to the same goal destination. Parallel parenting requires that parents have a common understanding of what each other are doing in their respective household with regards to the kids, and they ensure that what they are doing is similar. There is limited interaction or communication between parents, but children have predictability, structure and routine through their parenting time with both Mom and Dad.

Often parents that are using a parallel parenting model will have a written parenting plan, which is a document that outlines the various aspects of raising their children. Parenting plans will include details of the children's lives such as parenting time schedules (access and visitation in legal terms), routines, discipline, medical issues, supervision, and extra financial considerations for special events and even issues of daily routines and extracurricular activities for the children.

Communication between parents may be through attorneys, therapists or counselors, mediators or even via email if personal contact is still stressful. In most cases parallel parenting is beneficial to the children since they have security, routine and the understanding that Mom and Dad are working together in their upbringing and care.

CO-PARENTING

The most child friendly model of parenting through divorce is the model most commonly known as co-parenting. In this model Mom and Dad continue to discuss issues as they relate to the child or children, interact routinely with regards to information specific to the kids, and often talk and/or phone each other with questions or concerns about the kids. While parents may not specifically spend time together with the kids, many co-parents attend birthday parties, school events and other special activities together to allow the child to feel very much a part of both parent's lives.

Many people feel that co-parenting is an unreasonable expectation for divorced parents, however research clearly indicates that this is the best possible model for your children, provided both parents can remain civil, respectful and child centered during discussions and interactions. Co- parenting is almost like operating a business with the other parent as a partner with the goal of raising the happiest, healthiest kids. Co-parenting does not mean that you have to have extended conversations about anything other than the kids' health, happiness and general well being and development.

Co-parenting requires a lot of effort on both parent's part. Whatever caused the break up of the marriage has to be put aside or in the past, with all communication between the two parents now related to bringing up your children. Anger and frustration may occur, but effective co-parents use anger management and communication techniques to minimize or eliminate any anger towards each other in the presence of the children.

Chapter 5: How Parents' Involvement Affects Their Kids

Be it the simple way you ask them about their day or how you pack them lunch, your involvement in your kids' life affects them from their childhood years to adolescence, teenage years and all the way to adulthood. It affects how their views and philosophies in life, how they react to certain situations and how they handle problems.

Though too much attention and indulging kids is not always a good idea, too little also works negatively. It's best to have it balanced. You should know when to support them and when to reprimand them. But whichever you do, you have to make sure that your kids understand you.

Back in 2013, statistics show that almost a quarter of teenagers in America think that their parents do not have enough time for them. The ironic thing is when their parents were asked about it, they feel the exact opposite. This goes to show that there's a disconnection between the parent and the kid and that will cause a lot of problems in the future. It's very important that you and your kids sit down and talk about how much time they need from you and the amount of time you can give them.

There are different ways of getting involved in your kid's life. It doesn't always include attending recitals or helping them write their essays. Here are some ways parents' involvement affect their children:

Emotional Health – It's important for your kids to wake up every day and know that you're there for them. Be it a warm smile in the morning or a hug before they go to sleep, these gestures make your kids feel safe and wanted. Compared to children whose parents are barley home, kids who see their parent before they go to school and when they come home experience less emotional distress. Their emotional health is stronger and they perceive things better than others. So while your kids are still young, always remember to give them enough time every day. Be there when they wake up and be there before they go to sleep. Even occasionally tucking them in bed is heartwarming gesture that your kids will always remember. Just like Carl Buechner said, "They may forget what you said, but they will not forget how you made them feel."

Educational Attainment – It's very important for kids to know that their parents support their education not just financially but actively participating in teaching them about certain subjects. It makes a big difference when your kids also learn from you. Help them with their math assignment or give a hand in making that science project. Ask your kids if you can read their poems and essays. Give them comments and point out areas for improvement. Your kids will feel that you really value their education and monitor their progress. Kids whose parents are actively involved in their education tend to get higher grades and higher educational attainment. Teachers also report that there's a big progress when parents also participate in teaching their kids at home.

Self-Esteem – Aside from peer pressure, another determining factor of a child's self-esteem is the involvement of the parents in his or her life. When kids feel loved, wanted and an important member of a family, they feel secure and tend to develop and positive outlook in life. They get emotional support from their parents that even when there's peer pressure and bullying involved, these kids rarely breakdown. It's very important for your children to feel secure, especially during adolescence when their bodies start to change and they experience problems that affect their self-esteem. Let them know that you're there and talk to them about their problems. Open up to them and tell them about your teenage years. This way, they'll feel more comfortable talking to you when they know that you also went through similar situations.

Behavior – Parents' involvement in their children's lives are very evident in their behavior. Kids whose parents are actively involved in their activities are less aggressive, more outgoing and have good decision making skills. Their tendency to be involved in delinquent activities, smoking, substance abuse and teenage pregnancy is also lower.

Your involvement in your kids' lives affects them more than you think it does. It affects their self-esteem, their emotional health, their outlook in life and how they perceive themselves and others. It's very important to take into consideration that your kids need more than money and material things to survive. They need you the most.

Chapter 6: Secret To Being A Great Step Dad

In this modern age of blended families, it's not unusual to find yourself falling in love with a woman who has children from a previous marriage. You are not their father, but you still have some responsibility toward them because of your relationship with their mom.

Figuring out the best way to handle it, walking a fine line between stranger and family, can be difficult - for both you and for the kids.

There is a reason that the "wicked stepmother" is such a powerful image in children's literature. The idea of a new person coming in and taking the place of a beloved parent is scary for kids, and they can act out in all sorts of unpleasant ways.

It can make it difficult to show them the sort of love that they require - partly because it's tough for the stepparent to know just what is appropriate.

But even if parenting is an entirely new concept to you, there are a few things that you can remember:

1. Talk to the children's mother about your role.

In many households, the stepfather is given absolutely no say in disciplining the children. Sometimes it's because the mother doesn't want to give up the control of being the sole parental influence. Or it could be that it seems easier for all involved, so that arguments of the "you're not my dad" type can be side-stepped.

This decision is, of course, up to you and your wife. But part of being a good parent is fair, firm discipline, and if you aren't given any rights in this regard it can create real confusion and disharmony in your family.

Make the decision, instead, to discuss all matters of discipline between the two of you for awhile, and form a united front. That way, the kids will begin to see you as parent, too, and not just the new guy that Mom brought home.

2. Choose your battles wisely.

Children constantly test boundaries, doubly so with stepparents. It might start with a refusal to go to bed on time, or to turn down the stereo, or to help with dishes. After your requests have been ignored a few times, you may find yourself starting to get angry.

Take a step back and put it into perspective. Think about what will be more important a year - or five years - from now, having developed a relationship or getting the dishes done.

Your stepchildren are trying to find out what kind of person you are and what your relationship will be, and if you fly into a fury over a missed bedtime you'll reinforce all their worst fears about having a stepfather.

3. Be supportive and positive.

Congratulate your step kid when she gets a good grade on a test, and show interest in their lives and their schoolwork. Don't be surprised if they grumble or downplay the achievement - remember, they aren't sure how to act with you, either, but if you keep showing that you like and care about them, they'll appreciate it.

4. Recognize emotions, both theirs and your own.

Everybody has ups and downs, and they can be especially intense for children. Acknowledge that they'll be sad once in awhile, especially if there are visitation and custody issues between their mother and her ex. Respect their feelings just as you would want yours respected, and don't insist that they put on a big, fake smile all the time to "prove" they're happy.

The same goes for you - be emotionally honest, and don't try to be jolly all the time because you think that'll make for a happier family. Let your stepchildren get to know the real you, even when you're cranky, tired or stressed out.

Just don't take it out on them, and talk honestly about your feelings instead.

5. Put punishment into perspective.

Punishing mistakes or bad behavior is often the least effective technique for getting kids to behave. The most successful way to deal with potential problems is discuss with your wife ways to set reasonable expectations and what to do if they aren't met. Limiting television, Internet use and cellphone calls if homework isn't completed is one way to handle a problem.

Doling out "credit" for extra TV time if they do chores is another. Kids do best when they know what the rules are and what will happen if they don't fulfill their obligations - and it'll make it easier for you as a stepfather to enforce those rules if everyone has agreed on what they are.

The most important secret to being a good stepfather is simply to be patient and loving. Your role in the family will be established in time - in the beginning, just be the kindest, most giving person you can be, and you will soon find that your stepchildren accept you as a parent.

Chapter 7: Two Essential Parenting Traits

CARING

Parenting is, first of all, about **CARING**. Caring means love, kindness, compassion and helpfulness. Love and affection are the bedrock of healthy development. Kids know whether their parents care for them or not by the way they're treated – no surprise. This means more than just putting food on the table – adults are often distracted with so many other things, that we neglect daily interactions that are so essential, and so meaningful, to children. Not easy for any of us on some days!

The need for a positive, supportive home environment cannot be emphasized enough. Stress damages the development of the brain's architecture; and research shows that children who are subjected to mental, emotional and/or physical stresses for long periods of time are much more likely to experience mental illnesses and various types of depression – often leading to delinquency and incarceration – in addition to having more medical and marital problems. Toxic stress creates abnormal levels of stress hormones, resulting in often long-lived mental and physical impairments. So, pay close attention to your parenting skills…..

There is a difference, however, between the effects of long-term stress, and short-term stresses. You will likely know whether David will be more severely affected by the death of Buddy the dog, maybe because he's younger, quieter, and is more easily upset by events. But it's also imperative that you pay attention to the effects on Jason and Jill – i.e., Jason may have felt especially close to Buddy, and need extra support as well.

The way in which you counteract the effects of a sudden death, or any other traumatic event, is to take the time to help your children understand the event; and then give them more attention and affection for a while. Then when Grandpa passes away, they will already feel secure, and will come to you for comfort and support, increasing their emotional resilience – a critical capability for all of us.

Caring is not just a feeling, it is also about behavior. It means observing and learning about your children – their personalities, preferences, and foibles – and then consistently providing creative opportunities for them to grow physically, mentally, and emotionally. This does not require lots of stuff – in fact, too much stuff can be very inhibiting. It's really about actually listening to what your children say and responding with more than a distracted "Good." It means taking time, even if it's just a few minutes, to specifically focus on David, and on Jill, and on Jason as individuals.

Take conversations, for example. It's important for you to talk to your infants and toddlers, even when they don't seem to be paying attention. When you pay attention to them, and talk to them, it tells them that you care about them. (We even talk to our pets, knowing they don't understand the words, but most certainly understand our body language.)

This creates an emotional connection and makes them feel secure in their environment. Children who are emotionally secure are ready to learn — not only recognizing words, shapes and colors which will help them 'read' picture books and sight words, but also beginning to understand the uses of symbols — words — in reading and writing. On the other hand, children who are afraid or feel insecure do not learn nearly as well; and some will quickly fall behind.

Paying attention to them when they are doing things you want them to do also reinforces good behavior, since they don't have to tantrum to get your attention. This won't eliminate all tantrums, but will reduce the number and severity of them. Rewards for good behavior – attention, affection, polite conversations, an unexpected cookie bite when they're concentrating on a task – all of these reward effort and accomplishment, increasing self-esteem and confidence…important for all learning.

CARING is expressed by some very simple things:

Frequent displays of affection – quick hugs, patting heads, squeezing arms, high "5s."

Take care of basic needs for proper clothing, regular food, and safe spaces.

Provide emotional support when kids are sad, upset, or frustrated.

Spend time with them, and talking about things of interest to them.

Praise their efforts, and encouraging them to try new things.

Reward good behavior with praise, hugs, attention and affection.

CONSISTENT

Parenting is also about being CONSISTENT – consistent caring, consistent control, and consistent monitoring where needed. Children need to be cared for, given rules and structures for how to behave, along with being encouraged to explore the world on their own terms – consistently. This means daily, even hourly. (And yes, you can have bad days without ruining your kids.) Difficulties are ever-present, from finances to traffic jams to custody issues – and simply not having enough time in the day; but it takes moments, not hours, to convey love and caring.

Caring and Consistency are not about collecting stuff, and do not require any expensive food, toys, or clothing. There are thousands of websites that will sell the 'best' toys and the 'best' books and the 'best' games for making your child a musical genius or a mathematical prodigy. Believe it if you must, but don't fret if you don't have the money to buy all this stuff.

We know that creativity often begins with children taking sticks and rocks and discarded boxes and making up their own games. Mechanical toys break down; but simpler toys such as different sizes of building blocks, let kids make up their own structures – a creative, mind-building activity. Some toys such as Legos now have their own complex creations with step-by-step instructions – a very non-creative activity. This is not a step forward, in my view.

Being Consistent is somewhat like the basics of losing weight…all of us like to think that this type of tea or the newest diet pill will work its magic and make us lose 20 pounds without having to change our diet or exercise habits. Most of us have learned that it just ain't so, Joe.

We still have to pay attention to the basics of calorie control and good exercise if we expect to make any diet work for very long. The same applies to parenting….pay attention to the basics of caring and consistency through all the ups and downs, and your children will flourish.

CONSISTENCY simply means:

Establish structures that add stability and a sense of security to their routines. Your daily routine might include having breakfast together, after-school cookies, helping with dinner, doing homework, regular bedtime with stories and hugs.

Get them (and you) to school, church and other appointments on time, which teaches time management without lecturing.

Plan ahead by talking about their weekly and daily schedules, which develops and strengthens their executive functions of logic, planning and organization.

Allow for 'free' time to encourage independence and creativity.

Reduce nagging by letting them fail sometimes – i.e., no homework completed results in a failing grade, which means they can't stay over with a friend on Friday night.

You will note that there are many sources of free and low-cost information about good nutrition, food allergies, managing tantrums, and activities of all types. You can find them at the local library, on the Internet, and even free magazines and pamphlets in grocery stores.

If you don't have a computer at home, go to the library and (while your kids participate in a story-telling activity) use the library computers to search for parenting websites and magazines, local activities at parks, free days at museums, and other options close to you. There are also many parenting classes made available by schools and various other organizations – take advantage of them.

Chapter 8: What Is Depression?

While moodiness and extreme emotions are considered normal in most teenagers, there are times when it goes to the extreme. Your teenager is going to have times when they are down or sad, but when these start to become a part of their personality and they are never happy or excited about anything, you could be dealing with a teenager who is going through depression.

Depression is not the normal moodiness that you find in your teenager. Depression is considered a serious mental health problem that could lead to suicidal thoughts and other behaviors that are not good for your teenager. While it was long thought that teenagers and children couldn't get things like depression, it has been found that this thought process is not true and that many younger children and teenagers do suffer from these mental disorders.

Recognizing the signs of depression and that there is an issue for your teenager is the first step to helping them get the treatment that they need. But with the moodiness and other rebellion issues that many teenagers face, it is sometimes hard to figure out when they are suffering from depression or just from being a teenager.

Some of the signs that you should look for when you are worried about your teenager having depression include:

A mood that is cranky, empty, sad, and irritable and the belief in your teen that life is completely void of meaning.

Loss of interest in activities and sports that the teen used to really love. They will also withdraw from their family and friends and start to have issues with their relationships.

Changes in their appetite that include significant weight loss or gain

Lots of late night activities-going to the excess, with too little or too much sleep. Always running late for things because it is hard to get up in the morning.

Physical slowness and agitation. They may pace a lot and have repetitive and excessive behaviors

Loss of their energy, withdrawing from social interactions, boredom, and a refusal to go in with their usual activities.

Makes critical comments in regards to themselves, start to have issues at home or school, and have a sensitivity to rejection

Poor performance in their school work, missing school often, and their grades drop, especially if they used to do well in school.

Complaints of physical pain, such as pain in their stomach or headaches and they begin to visit the nurse at school more often.

Writing about dying, starting to give away some of their favorite belongings, and making comments about how others would be better without them there.

If you start to notice some of these comments and behaviors in your teenager, it is time to step in. These are not considered normal teenager moodiness and they are all signs of a serious issue. Often more than one of these signs are going to be present when your teenager is suffering from depression so pay attention and find out whether the behavior is typical for your teenager or if there is another issue at hand that needs some attention.

Chapter 9: How To Choose The Right Discipline Method

You are going to have to choose several different discipline techniques, depending on your child's behavior. As you probably already know, there is not a one-size-fits-all discipline technique; this means that you are going to have to have a few back-up plans for the different behaviors that your child regularly displays, as well as a plan for behaviors that do not occur on a regular basis. In order to do this, you have to understand your child's temperament, so that you can predict the way that your child will behave. This will ensure that you are ready with the proper discipline when it is needed.

There are several types of discipline from which you can choose. The first type is natural consequences. This is when you allow things to unfold naturally and allow the child to comprehend what happens when he displays a specific behavior. This is done only when the child is not in danger and can safely learn a lesson from what happens. One example of this is when a child keeps dropping his or her food, thinking that you will pick it up and give it back. Don't pick it up. Let the dog take the cookies and soon the child will understand that if he or she keeps dropping the cookies, there will be no more cookies.

If the child breaks his or her toy, let the child understand that he or she can no longer play with the toy and you will not be replacing the toy. Either the child will stop breaking his toys or he will soon find that he has no toys to play with. When this happens, children learn how to take care of what they have and become more grateful for what they have.

You have to remember that your child is going to learn more when he or she is allowed to learn naturally. Just as you have learned from your mistakes in life, you will have to allow life to discipline your child at some point.

Logical consequence is the next type of discipline that we are going to talk about; this is when you have to create a consequence for a behavior. You have to use logic when it comes to this discipline technique, meaning that the consequence has to directly relate to the behavior. For example, if your child refuses to pick up his or her toys, you can explain to the child that you will pick them up, but they will be off-limits to the child for the rest of the day. You have to stick to this, so make sure that it is something that you are willing to do. If you tell a child that he will not be allowed to play with his toys, and then you pick them up and an hour later give in and let him play with the toys, he will have learned nothing except that you do not do what you say you will do.

The next technique is **withholding privileges**. This is a technique that is often used on older children, but with all of the technology that children have access to today, this can be useful at any age. You need to make sure that if you are withholding privileges the discipline takes effect right at that moment. For example, if the child does not mind in the morning before going to daycare, you do not want to tell him that he is going to lose television privileges for that evening. This is because by the time evening comes, the child will have forgotten what he did that morning and will feel that he is being punished for no reason. Chances are you will have also forgotten about it, and there will be no consequence for the behavior after all.

Withholding privileges is very simple – all you have to do is take away something that your child likes when his behavior does not match what you want it to be. You have to take action immediately and make sure that he understands why he is being disciplined. The discipline also has to relate to the behavior. For example, if the child splashes in the bathtub, you do not want to take away his favorite stuffed animal. Instead, take away his bath toys to make bath time about getting clean and not about having fun. This helps children understand that when they do not behave properly, they do not get to have fun. It would also be a good idea to have your child clean up the mess that he has made, provided he is old enough to do this.

You never want to withhold something that your child really needs, such as food. Sending a child to bed without dinner is not discipline, and borders on abuse. Remember, you are taking away privileges – a meal is not a privilege, but a need.

Always ensure that you follow through. For example, if you threaten to take away a toy, make sure you take it away. You can hide the toy in your dresser drawer until the child is supposed to get it back, but make sure that you take the toy and that you do not give in and give it back before the lesson is learned.

Time-out is the next technique that I want to discuss. This is a technique that many people use, but often they do not use it effectively. In order to properly use the time-out method you have to make sure that the child knows the rules ahead of time. Start with two or three behaviors that you want to work on with your child, and let your child know that breaking these rules will result in a time-out.

Choose a spot that the child will go to during the time-out. Make sure that this spot does not have stimuli for the child, such as access to television, toys, or other entertainment. Show this space to your child and explain to him that this is the area he will go to when he breaks one of the rules.

The child should spend one minute in time-out for each year of his age. In other words, if the child is four years old he or she should spend four minutes in time-out after breaking the rule. This is a continuous amount of time, which means that if the child moves from the area the time starts over.

We will talk more about time-out later as it is one of the best ways to discipline a child and ensure that he has time to calm down.

Finally, **physical intervention** is the last technique. This is done only when the child is in danger – for example, if the child wanders out into the road. Grab your child out of the dangerous situation, explain to him that he cannot do whatever it was he was doing, as well as what could happen to him. You do not have to worry about any other form of discipline because the fear itself should teach the child not to repeat the behavior in the future. If the behavior is repeated, you may choose to add in another type of discipline.

Chapter 10: How Do Parents Communicate Effectively With A Toddler?

Tips for Communicating With Your Toddler Good communication is necessary for any relationship, especially for those whom you are closest to. More specifically, it is important to communicate with your children, especially when they are toddlers, to have an effective relationship. Sometimes it may seem difficult to communicate with your toddler, because at times it may seem that they are speaking an entirely different language. And sometimes, this is true. See below a few tips which can help you and your child to communicate more effectively.

Keep It Simple

It is difficult for children to follow many directions given at one time. Also, keep in mind that your child's vocabulary is not as vast as yours may be. This means do not confuse your child by speaking to them in a language that they do not understand. Instead, keep it simple. This means using language your child understands. Try speaking in short brief sentences and be clear and concise with what you are trying to say. Try to be as simple as possible without resorting to "baby talk."

Be Realistic

Do not have expectations for your child that they could not achieve, instead your expectations should be more realistic. Your toddler is not going to be able to understand and say all the things you may want them to. So, do not expect them to. When your child asks you something, take a minute before you respond. Try to put yourself in their shoes and then respond. This will allow your response to be much more simple and easier for your child to understand.

Have a Positive Tone of Voice

Children have an uncanny ability to tell when their parents are not in a good mood or are frustrated. This is why it is important to speak to your child a calm and positive voice. Try to avoid negative remarks such as "I'm so mad at you right now" or "you're acting like a baby." These types of comments only exacerbate the situation. When you speak to him/her in a more positive manner, your child is more apt to listen and to be able to understand what you are saying to them. Also, this will teach your child a very valuable lesson. It will teach them to speak to others kindly and respectfully and learn how to communicate effectively without using negative comments.

Lead By Example

This is one of the more important tips on communicating effectively with your child. If your child sees you speaking to someone a certain way, then they are more likely to speak to others in the same way. A lot of what children learn, even in the way of communicating, they pick up from watching their parents. This means that the parent needs to be mindful of how they speak to others in front of their child. This not only affects how they communicate with others, but also how they will communicate with their parents as well.

Make Sure Your Child Understands

When explaining something to your child, make sure that he/she understands what you are saying. Ask your child to repeat back to you what you just told them. If your child cannot repeat what you told them or doesn't understand, then try explaining it to them differently with shorter and more concise sentences.

Get On Their Level

When speaking to your child, it is important to literally get on their level. This means that you should get low enough in order to make eye contact with your child when you speak to them. This will help you to make sure that your child is focusing on what you are saying to them, which will help to ensure they understand you as well. Making eye contact will also let your child know that he/she has your undivided attention. This lets them know that you are paying attention to and listening to them.

Say Their Name

When speaking to your child say their name. It is a lot easier to get your child's attention when you call their name. This works a lot better at getting their attention if they are doing something wrong then just shouting at them. If you really want to get your child's attention if they are causing trouble then use their name, and use it firmly.

Listen to Them

If your child is trying to explain something to you, then listen. Do not continue to interrupt them in the middle of their story. Treat your child in this situation, as you would want anyone else to treat you. This will also let your child know that they should give others the same type of respect.

Open-Ended Questions

When asking your child questions, make sure that they are open-ended questions. This means don't ask them questions where the only possible answer is yes/no; you want to ask them questions that require an actual explanation, which allows your child to share their ideas, emotions and feelings.

Schedule Some One on One Time

Make sure you take time out of your day to sit down and talk to your child. This may be especially important if you have a busy lifestyle. It is important to take this time to talk to your child, either after dinner or before bed.

Don't Yell At Your Child

This is probably the most important tip to ensure effective communication between you and your toddler. When you are trying to communicate with a toddler, the last thing you want to do is yell. This will almost certainly cause him/her to cry and they will not be listening to what you are trying to say. Instead, try to maintain a calm tone of voice. This will help tremendously in communicating with your child.

Toddlers are emotional people. It is difficult to communicate with them effectively because of this. However, if you utilize some of these tips it may help bridge the communication gap between you and your child.

Chapter 11: Aggressive Behaviour

Aggression is a reactionary, unplanned, and impulsive behaviour that usually results from feelings of anger, fear, or the need to retaliate against another person. Aggressive behaviour can be triggered by multiple situations such as; your child not getting what they want from the shops, not wanting to sit in their car seat, fighting with siblings, not wanting to go to bed or just outright disagreeing with you.Anger is destructive and can cause emotional or physical harm to family members and others, intentionally or unintentionally.

Understanding Aggression

Aggression can be a problem for children with healthy development as well as those who are suffering from psychosocial disturbances. The harm done to someone through accidents isn't considered as resulting from aggression since aggression involves the perception of intent. For instance, if your child accidentally breaks someone's arm during a rugby match, that won't qualify as aggressive behaviour, since he did not intend any harm.

Social isolation, changes in the home environment and underlying health conditions can lead to increased aggression in children. Also, the level of hostility shown by a child depends on their sex. As such, it's proven that boys are more aggressive than girls. Some children, regardless of age group, are aggressive because they found out that aggression is a powerful way to communicate their wishes. Others see it as the only way to handle their likes and dislikes. For example, infants tend to be aggressive when they are hungry, angry, fearful, in pain, or uncomfortable.

You can tell what your child needs by their loudness and pitch of crying. Some even thrash their arms and legs as a way of communicating their feelings and needs. Similarly, it is not uncommon to find children between ages 2-4 showing aggressive behaviour such as damaging furniture, toys, hurting others, or throwing temper tantrums due to frustration. Some children see attacking others as a way of standing up for themselves.

The following factors can cause aggressive behaviour in children:

- **Stress**
- **Frustration**
- Inability to express feelings
- Being ignored
- Angry feelings
- Poor relationship skills
- Hurt (physically or emotionally)
- Health conditions
- Use of drugs and alcohol
- Peer influence
- Being attacked (physically or verbally)
- Exposure to violence (whether at home, socially or in the media)

Dealing with Anger

Parents are encouraged to use violence prevention strategies to dramatically reduce their children's exposure to violence in the home, in the community, as well as in the media. The more violence your child becomes exposed to at a young age, the more they consider it acceptable behaviour. Next time your child gets angry, try the below to see if you can reduce the anger in your child:

•Make every effort to stay calm regardless of how irksome the situation is. Speak respectfully and try your best to understand your angry child.

•Do not become aggressive yourself and resist the urge to yell at your child. Through all the screaming and crying your child is trying to communicate with you.

•Accept your child's feelings, even if you consider them to be inconvenient or do not agree with the reasons behind the anger. Always resist the urge to deny your child to their feelings. Let your child know that it is okay to feel what they are feeling and that you can assist them in identifying whatever it is they are having trouble with.

When you acknowledge your child's anger and frustration, you prove to them that you are listening and understand how they feel.

•Give your child the freedom to express themselves. Being angry doesn't make your child a horrible person. It only shows that they do not yet know the appropriate ways to express their feelings. To overcome this, try and encourage your child to express their feelings through communication. If your child refuses to talk about their feelings, don't force it. Allow them to express it how they deem fit, but set limits. With time, they will learn, grow and adjust.

Chapter 12: Potty Training

Potty and toilet training your toddler is an important aspect of parenting. Imagine what it would have been like if your parents had not potty trained you? You have to, therefore, make an effort to train your child and ensure that he/she is able to use the toilet independently.

In order to toilet train, there are a few basic steps to follow that are as shown below:

●**Step 1**: The first step of the process is to introduce your child to the potty. Children will be used to the diaper and find it a little tough to make the transition. The best thing will be to show them the potty chair and explain what it is used for. Buying a colorful one will help garner their attention. It should be comfortable for them to sit on and fit them correctly.

●**Step 2**: The next step is to look if they are ready for training. Many parents do not understand that toddlers have to be ready for potty training and force them to transition too early. Forcing them if they are not ready will not work out well and your child will begin to hate the training. It would, therefore, be best to wait for some signs that will tell you whether or not your toddler is ready. The first sign will be to check if your toddler tugs at the diaper to showcase discomfort. This is the sign that he/she is ready to use the potty. The next sign will be to see if they remove the diaper by themselves. The third sign will be to see if they themselves run to the bathroom when they wish to relieve themselves. This will tell you that your toddler is ready to undergo potty training.

•**Step 3**: The next step is to gently place your baby on the potty chair. Pick him/her up and gently place them down on the chair. Ensure that you place the chair in a room that they like so that they will stay put. Try to do away with distractions in the room as they can distract him/her and make them want to get up. Sit by their side and hold their hand so that they feel comfortable. It will be ideal to remove every bit of clothing from the waist down on your toddler, as he/she will be more comfortable.

●**Step 4**: It will be ideal to set a schedule for training, as it will help the toddler learn better. Try to train the toddler at the same time every day, ideally during the mornings. After some time the child will start to run to the potty chair without your help. Be ready to run with your baby so that the child places him/herself correctly on the potty chair.

●**Step 5**: The next step will be to move them from the potty chair to the toilet seat. For this, you have to slowly move their potty towards the toilet through the course of a week or two. Once they are ready, gently place them over the seat and hold their hands. Most toilet seats will be quite big for them so ensure that you place them correctly. You have to show them the correct way to sit down on the toilet by demonstrating it. Once they get accustomed to it, you still have to be with them for some more time so that they get used to it. Teach them to flush every time. You may want to place something they can use as a step in front of the toilet for easy access.

●**Step 6**: It will be extremely important for you to teach your toddler about hygiene. Babies and toddlers will not be aware of the importance of this and should be fostered from a young age. Accustom them to using the tissue/paper to clean themselves then make sure they are paying attention when you clean them, in order to do it correctly. They should not be distracted or they may not understand what you are teaching them. Teach them to wash their hands every single time that they use the toilet.

●**Step 7**: In the beginning, you should offer your child a reward each time they use the potty successfully so that they understand the value of obeying a command and being successful in their attempts. The reward can be a toy or a treat of your choice. But it has to be lucrative enough to help them listen to you.

●**Step 8**: Pee training will be different for boys and girls. For boys, you will have to teach the toddler to aim correctly into the toilet bowl. For girls, you should place them correctly over the toilet so that the child pees inside it. If you have to train a son and a daughter, then separate them, as otherwise they will get confused looking at each other. Go with them to the toilet every time they have to relieve themselves to ensure that they are doing it correctly.

Remember to always keep an eye on your child while potty training, as children, can get curious and start playing with the poop. If that happens then be strict with him/her and firmly say "NO." If you have an older child who is potty trained, then you can get him or her to help you train the younger one. Children tend to listen better to their siblings and will learn faster.It will be a good idea to use toys and books as a means to show them the importance of potty training and teach them. Showing them YouTube videos will also help you train them easily.

Chapter 13: Toddler Tantrum And Hissy Fit Solutions

Toddler tantrum is always a difficult situation and condition that no parent ever desires it. The effects are mostly felt by first-time parents who do not know what it is like. The question is why is toddler tantrum extremely difficult for parents mostly first-time parents to handle? The reason for this is always that parents often see it as a responsibility to make toddlers behave the way they think and desire for them to behave. But, the reverse is always the case due to tantrum which usually makes most parents to even find it difficult holding themselves, so they will not have a meltdown along the line. First-time parents are always concerned about the judgment made around them when their toddlers are in the middle of a tantrum. That normally makes them feel ineffective to control and coordinate their toddlers even in the middle of a tantrum.

The truth is that toddlers within 1-3 years have not learned how to manage their frustration, which is the reason for the tantrum. So, the more parents wish for their toddler to behave normally in public, the more frustrated they will become. That can be linked to the reason why most parents usually have their own meltdown or tantrum when they are in such a difficult situation. Getting into your own tantrum can only fuel the situation and make matters worse. That is why for the first time parents, they should learn to control themselves, control their emotions and never to allow their ego push them into rage against their tantrum toddler. The first solution to toddler tantrum is to try dealing with your own feeling of frustration, embarrassment, and happiness when toddlers are in the middle of a tantrum.

Most first time parents have asked several times whether there is a way to prevent toddler tantrum from happening. The answer has always been no as toddler tantrums have been regarded as the phase of life every child has to pass through. It is a normal thing that can come up at any point in time no matter how good or caring you are to your children. In fact, even the adult usually have tantrums all the time by losing their temper even in the middle of a conversation with a friend, family or colleague. The only thing different is that normal adults have learned how to cope with the situation and manage meltdown, so it will not really be so obvious or disturbing to people around, which is part of maturity. There are basically six toddler tantrum and hissy fit solutions presented in this Ebook.

1.Maintain your principles: Being about holding yourself when your toddler is having a tantrum in public is really important. One of the best ways to achieve this is to be ready to hold up to your principles. In your own quiet moment, try to think of how you will like to handle worst toddler tantrum. Consider the most appropriate way to handle your emotion in the face of worse provocation from your tantrum toddler. Make sure you hold that as your principle and try to reflect on it when your child happens to be in a tantrum and try to maintain it. This may require practice, but it will really be of great importance if you can do it.

2.Try to avoid anything that can trigger toddler tantrums: Though things that result to toddler tantrums are not always predictable, but you can try to learn the situations that usually result to it.You can try to teach your child the new way of doing things next time he is provoked to throw a tantrum. Also, you have to do every possible thing to avoid physical triggers. You can do this by making sure your toddler is having proper sleep and rest and also ensure you provide her with food at the appropriate time. Your ability to do this will help you avoid tantrum in your toddler. However, you should not always provide your toddler with all the things she wants to avoid making her think that is the best way to live.

3.Make sure you plan ahead and be yourself: It is important for you to always plan ahead for your toddler tantrum. You can do this by telling the child what you expect when you are in the supermarket with her. Teach the toddler how to manage frustration that may arise while both of you are in the supermarket and what you will do if she happens not to manage the frustration as you advised. Just make sure you stick to your plan and do just as you already told her while at home. It can be just putting your hand on the child to take her out of the supermarket.

4.Be Realistic about things you can handle: Being realistic about things you can handle when it comes to toddler tantrum is a good step to solving the problem. Since you already know some things that usually trigger frustration at your child you can tell her beforehand and allow her to show you how she can avoid that.

5. Always be in control of your emotion: This is one of the most vital solutions to toddler tantrum. You need to always be in absolute control of your emotions and actions. That will help you to avoid fueling your toddler tantrum through your own meltdown. To put yourself under control while your child is in the middle of a tantrum, you can just walk around your house, pick up the phone and call your friend or simply take a time out to ensure that your own mind is calmed and settled. This will go a long way in shortening the duration for the toddler tantrum.

6. Show good examples to your toddler: One thing all first-time parents should know is that toddlers are observing their actions than words. How you react to provocations and frustration will determine how your toddler will react while in the middle of a tantrum. So, instead of consistently yelling at your

tantrum toddler, you have to show her a `good example by controlling your own anger. In fact, by asking how you can calm your tantrum toddler down, you should also ask how you can calm yourself down when your toddler is unable to do that.

Reasons why Your Toddler has Tantrums

There are several reasons for toddler tantrum, and that differ from one child to another. Your ability to identify the reason why your toddler is having tantrums will help you in managing the situation. For you to find out the possible reasons for toddler tantrum, you will need to take a close observation of the child for some time. Learning about reasons for toddler tantrum is not always easy for first time or frustrated parents. So, some of the generally observed reasons are:

The feeling of inadequacy

Frustration due to inability to express oneself through word

Inability to control their emotions

Jealousy

Lack of what they desire

Negative self-talk

Negative thought wandering in their mind

The feeling of inadequacy can come in the form of not being about to strengthen their bent straw while eating dinner with you in a restaurant. The frustration can easily be in not being able to talk properly and communicate their mind to adult. In fact, this is among the major reasons for toddler tantrum. They want to say something but find it difficult to say it, or they are even saying it, but their minder or parent is not paying enough attention to hear them out. Your toddler can develop the feel of jealousy when he discovers that you are treating the sibling better than you are treating him. Also, if a toddler sights something in a store like ice cream, cake or others but the parent refuses to get it for him, it can trigger a tantrum. Negative self-talk can result to outburst in toddlers. This is mostly when they begin to nurse some feelings within them and start having feelings of deprivation. They can also start to think negatively of themselves and their inability to do certain things like others.

8 Steps to Help a Toddler Learn How to Control Their Emotions and Refrain From Negative Behavior, Including Tantrums, Whining, And Sibling Rivalry

Anger management is not an easy thing even for an adult with several years of practice. Toddlers or preschoolers, who are only learning emotions, usually find it difficult to keep their anger under control. That is the reason why they usually get harsh on people that trigger their anger or responsible for their frustration. Some toddlers usually end up whining at people around, calling names and even throwing anything they have in their hands at the fellow. In most cases, some toddler tantrum usually results to sibling rivalry which can be violent if not controlled. It is important for you to know that understanding emotion and learning to manage anger is a continuous process.That is why as a first time or frustrated parent the best thing to do is to teach the toddlers how to identify things that usually trigger their frustration or rage. That will help them to also learn how to checkmate their own anger and emotion. This can be an effective way to manage tantrums and other anger related issues.

Indeed, there are eight steps to help a toddler learn how to control their emotions and refrain from negative behavior, including whining, tantrums, and sibling rivalry.

Find Out thought that triggers tantrum: There is always thought that comes before the outburst of anger in toddlers. If you are able to arrest the thought and change it from negative to positive, it will go a long way in helping your toddler learn to control her emotions and stay away from negative behavior. Negative thinking can result in concurrent anger outburst and unacceptable behavior if you do not teach her how to manage the thinking and change it to a positive one. You can easily start this by helping your toddler figure out the thought in her mind that triggered the anger. Most time the thought are centered on the inadequacy of the child, fear, jealousy and even anger.

Reduce the potential: There is always something that results in the frustration and emotional distress in the mind of your toddler before tantrum can set in. So, as first-time parents, your assignment should be to find out what normally triggers the anger of your toddler and try as much as possible to reduce it. You can suspend the activity that usually results to your toddler tantrum until she learns how to manage her anger or just stop it completely. If you know the game that usually leads to anger and sibling rivalry among your children, you can suspend that or only allow that when an adult is with them. Also, you can easily replace a particular situation that is causing a problem with another that is less problematic. Though there are unavoidable children activities that can result to anger like doing math homework, others can easily be avoided like a certain game.

Positive mental talking: If you are able to figure out the things that usually trigger anger in the mind of your toddler, the next thing should be to teach positive self-talk.Though children usually find it difficult to learn positive mental talking, it is always an effective way to avoid things that will trigger their anger. It is the best way to position their mind in the positive direction thereby helping them to refrain from things that usually cause an outburst of anger and rage. Constructive self-talk can help your toddler avoid situations that result to tantrum, whining, and even sibling rivalry. If she is defeated in baseball while playing with a sibling instead of feeling inadequate, jealous or thinking that the sibling is showing off, she can start thinking that she is good at the game and will win the sibling someday.

Teach them how to diffuse the anger: Individuals are different when it comes to things that help diffuse anger in their mind. Some toddlers can calm down when they go back to their room, listen to music or even take a walk out. Just identify the one that works for your toddler and teach her to always use it when there is outburst or tantrum instead of whining.

Tell others about your plan: Communicating your plans in calming your toddler tantrum is also an effective method to use. If you have discovered that your toddler normally gets tensed up or feel frustrated while in math class, you have to communicate that to the teacher. Telling your toddler's teacher about your plan to handle the outburst and also request for the teacher's assistant will go a long way in helping the situation.

Come up with a simple plan: Toddlers can easily start feeling embarrassed, overwhelmed or even angry when they start to experience difficult situations. It can be poor performance in the gym or even math class. Helping the child figure out a simple plan to getting the solution will work wonders. Let the child try to work out the one or two simple plans ahead of time, so he can apply it when the need arise.

Implement the set-out plan: Make sure the toddler implement the simple plan you helped him to make. The earlier the plan is used, the more effective it will likely be. The reason for the immediate implementation of the plan is to avoid forgetfulness which can always be the case. Also, you do not have to wait till your child's behavior start getting out of hand before implementing the simple plans you set out.

Teach the child how to move on: Trying a plan without getting adequate result can be frustrating to a toddler. But, you can teach him or her to move on even when the plan did not work. Whether the plan works or not, just let the child know that the best thing is to move on.

Chapter 14: Communication Is Crucial For Divorced Couples With Children

Getting a divorce means you will no longer be with the person you once thought you were going to spend the rest of your life with; however, you cannot divorce your children, therefore you are now in the situation of divorce and parenting.Many divorces are bitter and hurtful; however, spouses should make every effort to move past it for the sake of the children. Both parents should take and active role in the lives of the children and this can only be accomplished through effective communication. Both parents should participate in school functions as well as keep track of the children(s) classroom progress.

In the presence of children parents should be civil and make every effort to get along with each other especially as it relates to them.Neither parent should talk bad about the other in the presence of the children(s). Children should never be made to fell like they have to make a choice between their parents. In many instances divorced couples communicate with their ex-spouse through the children which places an undue burden on them. If face to face interaction is difficult then stick to communicating over the phone and keep it civil if the children are around. Try to keep an open line of communication and remember that compromise is very important when dealing with issues related to the children. Some divorces couples find that written communication works best since it prevents emotions from immediately dictating the conversation.

The communication will become strenuous at times but every effort to keep an even tone for the benefit of the children. It may be a good idea to attend a class with the ex-spouse to understand the importance of good communication after the divorce. You can also learn effective techniques to use going forward so the transition of divorce becomes more amiable. It can take some time to make this work but don't give up on it.

Classes For Divorcees With Children

Divorce is inevitable in some cases and the children deserve the right to a happy life after the divorce. Attending classes maybe the perfect opportunity to help start the healing process, strengthening the bonds and connections between parents and kids, individually and collectively as parents are living in separate households. One of the main objectives of these classes is to make sure each of the parents stay involved with their children. Statistics have revealed that that less than five years after a divorce more than half of all children are only in contact with one of their parents. Poor communication is one of the major facts that prevent the adults from effectively working together for the benefit of their children.

The majorities of divorcees are great parents and want what is best for their children. Enrolling in classes can help them to be a positive influence for their children. Divorce can be more difficult on children than many parents imagine because it can affect how they will form their own relationships even in adulthood. Generally the classes are flexible and most likely there will be one to accommodate the schedules of both spouses.Take time to find out which classes better suites your needs.

The class will help parents to understand how the children may be affected by the divorce and minimize the trauma within their lives. Although each child will be affected differently by divorce the spouses need to be ready to handle any situation that may arrive.The ultimate objective of the class is to have effective tools for raising children in separate homes.A divorce is an extremely difficult process and such classes have proven to make the process easier in many cases.

Never Use Children To Gain An Advantage In A Divorce

If children are an integral part of a divorce, then, the spouses have to remain in contact with each other. The children should never be used as pawns during or after the divorce because they are the ones that suffer for it. Some divorced parents try to punish each other by preventing one or the other from seeing the children. This type of action only punishes the children because they are the one's missing out on the relationship(s). In fact this should only be pursued if one of the parents is unfit to have visitation rights with the children alone.

Children have unconditional love for both of their parents and feel an absence and void when one of the parents has left from the home so parents should not play with their emotions. Children should have the flexibility to call the other parent when they miss them or even as a standard ritual before bed can help to relieve their anxiety. Parents should make sure all important sensitive details are discussed privately and never in the presence of the children.Children naturally need to know what is going on as far as the divorce is concerned; however, they don't need to know all of the details. When issues arise that involving the children, parents should work together to resolve them and never offer opposite solutions just to be difficult, it only hurts the children more. Sometime one parent will think that an issue is a bigger deal then the other; however, try to resolve it without making it ongoing.Children are going to want to follow the guideline of the parent that is in their favor so compromise is very much in order.Make every effort not to use your children as a pawn to drive your ex-spouse crazy; so find ways to work as a team to do what is in the best interest of the children.

One important rule of thumb is to never under any circumstances pass messages to your ex-spouse through your children. That isn't the children's responsibility and often times are told things they don't want to repeat. When the children are in the presence of either spouse it is not proper under any circumstance for them to ask questions like "what the other spouse "said" "who was around" or no other similar details. If either parent is having a hard time coming to terms with the divorce then they should seek professional counseling. This will help to work through the emotions and set goals for the future. Also you want to be able to have a good life be there for your children In a positive way and not dwell on what has taken place in the past.Finally make sure you always stop to consider how our actions are going to affect your children before you engage in them.

Chapter 15: Family Activities You Can Do Outdoors For Exercise

In our modern world, it is so important to teach our children to get outdoors and have some fun in the sun.Whether it means getting out into the backyard for a swim in the pool during the summer or to play games with siblings, friends, or even parents, or going hiking in a forest, the natural world stimulates creativity and is a perfect arena for exercising every part of a growing child's body.

You should encourage your children to get off the computer, away from the television, and off the cell phone as much as possible.These devices are distracting and entice children to lead sedentary lives with minimal social interaction.Instead, children should begin, from a very young age, to explore the outdoors, enjoying the sights, sounds, and smells of nature and all of its creatures, while learning to appreciate the natural environment, its delicate ecosystems, and its myriad forms of life.

As a family, you can encourage this kind of behavior by setting up days to play outside as a group. If you have a large family with many relatives, invite them over for a sporting event at the park, such as a soccer match or a softball game. Your children can even invite their friends to the events if they want to.

If your children are facing a high level of stress from school or from peers, take them for a calming walk, when they can rest their minds for a bit, rejuvenate, and talk out their problems with you in a very special bonding experience.

Ways to Pick the Healthiest Snacks from the Junk Food that Fills Stores

Getting children to eat healthy in a world filled with junk food and advertisements for fast food, poor quality meat and dairy products, and high-sugar foods can be extremely difficult.

Begin feeding your child, from as early as possible, foods that are healthy and contribute to strong bones and a strong immune system. Children pick up their eating habits from their parents, so be sure to set a good example so that they can follow your lead. Feeding your toddler fresh fruits and vegetables will help him/her acquire a taste for these foods. Once your child is used to eating healthy, and actually enjoys doing so, he/she will take these lessons into adulthood.

When it comes to picking snacks while you are at the supermarket, go for things that will not only contribute to long-lasting health, such as fresh, wholesome, colorful fruits and vegetables of all kinds, but will also provide sustained energy to power your children through their busy days at school and at their extra-curricular activities, such as nuts and legumes.

There are even chips made from vegetables, dried greens that can be eaten like chips, and other packaged snacks that are healthy but easy to take with you on the go.Peanut butter is also great for protein and energy, so use it on fruits, crackers, or whole wheat bread.Avoid chocolate, which contains caffeine that is not healthy for a growing child, as well as snacks that contain a lot of sugar, artificial dyes and flavors, and preservatives.

Chapter 16: Let Kids Be Themselves

How many times do we allow our children to make their own choices? Do we let them solve their own problems? Allowing our children to think for themselves is a hard concept for us to understand and to grasp. Parents often make the assumption that allowing their children to make choices and then allowing them to deal with the consequences start at an older stage. But how will it happen then? Children must learn from a very young age to make their own decisions. The earlier you start allowing your child to choose, display his or her feelings (good or bad) and respecting those choices, the better the relationship between parent and child will be.

Demonstrate with your own behavior how to make choices

By doing so, you teach your child to think for himself and to make his own decisions. Stand behind the choices you make and express your reasons for making them, which will help them understand why you chose the way you did.

Allow time to play freely

Unobstructed play is crucial to raising children to think for themselves. It is important in child development as it forces them to decide what to play and how to play. Start with building blocks when your child is very young.

Give your child the opportunity to express herself and her opinions

This must be done even if they run counter to yours. They may be immature opinions, or not completely well-thought out, but by encouraging exploration, you will encourage her to see the strengths and weaknesses in theories and arguments.

Let your child in on what you're thinking and how you're thinking about it

Communicate your own struggles, explorations, the moment when the "light bulb" went on, and how you work out problems.

Read up on ways to help your child develop critical-thinking skills

There are many good books on the topic, many of which include thought-provoking exercises, questions or tasks.

Be consistent in your approach.

Incorporate critical-thinking opportunities naturally into everyday life. Don't save it all up for a once-a-month critical-thinking lesson.

Let your children make small choices.

Let them choose between 2 or 3 outfits and let them wear it. As they build confidence with these small decisions, you can go on with larger choices. Like input on where to go for vacation.

Don't criticize the choices your children make.

Don't let your children feel guilty about their decisions. It will cause them to be insecure about the next decision they need to make.

Try not to make judgments or offer unsolicited opinions about situations your children find themselves in.

If they hear your thoughts or advice, they may feel as if they need someone else to tell them what to think or feel. Rather ask them what they think about the situation and what they believe the choices are. Encourage them to talk about what decision they want to make and why they want to make it.

Explain the rules in your house or in their school.

By doing this your children will be encouraged to decide to follow them, because they will understand them.

Discipline your children when they make bad choices.

When they make bad choices, inform them which actions you are disappointed with and why, and what the consequences are. Use simple wording whenever possible to make it easier for your children to concentrate on their actions.

Focus on the bad decisions or behavior, and not on the children themselves.

Try not to tell them that they are bad or wrong, and rather use words like: "your behavior is out of line". This prevents children from feeling personally attacked, and helps them understand that it is their actions you are not happy with, and not them.

Follow through on discipline: Your children need to learn that there are consequences for their actions and that making the wrong choice will lead to an appropriate punishment.

Don't threaten or bribe your children.

Using rewards or threats to influence their decisions will send a message that they are not capable of making good decisions without your help.

Trust and respect your children.

After you've laid the groundwork, give them room to make choices, and don't interfere unless there is danger. Sure, they will make bad decisions along the way, but in order to get better at the process, they need to have the freedom to do so.

Encourage lots of imaginative and free play.

Make time for wandering outside, exploring a woody path or creek bed.

Nurture curiosity.

Help your child follow his natural interests. Help him learn to gravitate toward positive activities and areas of interest that he likes and that give him satisfaction and enjoyment.

Ask questions and encourage questions.

Ask: "What do you think?" "What would you do in that situation?" Try to avoid simple yes-and-no questions/answers. Go for the "why."

Challenge your child to figure out more than one answer or option to a problem or challenge.

Teach her how to brainstorm, to come up with ideas that may not work but that aren't instantly shut down.

Teach decision-making skills.

This involves researching, creating pro/con lists, evaluating choices and anticipating consequences. Then your child the chance to "own" some of his own decisions.

Let your child experience the consequences of his actions.

He will begin to figure it out for himself.

Teach and model the value of calculated risk taking.

Trying new things is a form of positive experimentation. If it works out, your child learns the value of taking a chance and learns not to fear change. If it doesn't work out, she's learned a lesson as well. Try and you may succeed. Don't try, and you'll be stuck in a rut.

Expose your child to adults with a passion and energy for their work or hobbies.

This is modeling at its best. If you live in a metropolitan area or near a university, it's not hard to find speakers and workshops. If these aren't available, many great DVDs and television shows feature people with a passion for their work or hobbies. Ask friends to talk about or demonstrate their hobby or work to your child.

Some "Don'ts" ...

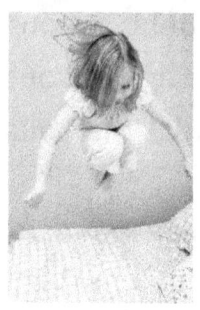

Hover.

Don't hang over your child's shoulder at every moment. Give her room for trial and error, to learn from her mistakes. Let her create something less than perfect. The lesson is often in the process, not the result.

Fall into the trap of passive entertainment.

Don't, let your children watch too much television or play too much on their iPods. If they love film or music, get them a cheap camcorder, sign them up for a class or encourage them to take up an instrument.

Over-structure a day.

If your child says, "I'm bored," don't automatically provide a list of things-to-do; challenge her to come up with fun ideas.

Rely on rote learning or memorization.

Get your child to understand the "why" of any project or activity.

Just say "no."

Frame the situation in questions that help the child figure out why something is either a good idea or not such a good idea. Example: Your child asks, "Can I go away with a friend for two weeks this summer?" You know she can't, but you want her to figure it out for herself. Have her come up with a list of pros and cons so she can begin to see the answer and possible solutions.

Chapter 17: Tips For Building Self Esteem

Poor self-esteem is characterized by someone feeling that they are of no importance and that they do not fit in the society. If you want your child to live a happy and fulfilling life, you need to build in them self-confidence and a sense of self-worth. A child who has self-esteem issues usually believes that they are a disappointment to those around them and this may lead them to depression and having suicidal thoughts. Self-esteem issues also resort to drug and alcohol abuse as well as binge-eating leading to weight gain and health problems. If your child lacks self-confidence, they will always feel inferior and lack empowerment to be productive in the society. Self-esteem also has to compliment your child's character. For example, exceptional leaders are likely to have good character and for them to stand in front of a group of people, they need to have a sense of self-worth. In order to ensure that you bring up children with self-esteem, we will look at some essential parenting tips.

Show Love And Support

From the time your child is born to when they are a toddler, when they start going to school and when they become teenagers, you need to constantly show them love and support. Without these, your child will feel that they are not wanted. You need to understand that children measure their own value by how other people perceive them. If they fail at a football game, they will see themselves as losers. Ensure that your child believes that you value him because of who he is, not how he performs. Don't expect your child to excel in sports or music or academics just because you did. The one thing your child can excel in is being themselves. Therefore, your child must know that your love for them does not depend on your approval of their performance.

Build Confidence

How a child feels about him or herself affects how they act. A confident child is able to stand up for him or herself when being harassed, make class presentations and excel in both social and academic work. The ability to excel boosts up their self-esteem in no time. You can also look for areas where your child does their best and compete with them ensuring that you let them defeat you in the game. A game of Chess can be a good one to practice on building your child's self-esteem.

Never make the mistake of comparing your child with other children, as this will dampen their spirits. In fact, tell them that they are more beautiful, clever and hardworking while also making sure that they don't end up being proud

Reward Efforts Made

Praise tactics work well for children; they love to receive praises for the little they have done from washing their face to tying up shoelaces. It is the little things we do to our children that make them value themselves. An act of kindness is crucial in building your child's self-esteem. Children show unconditional love and trust to parents as they look up to them. When they do something for you to reward them with some candy, toys or other gifts, they will not forget this and will feel good about themselves. However, rewards should not be material things only because we don't want our children to think that material things are what brings fulfillment.

Learn To Listen

Listening to your child is important to building their self-esteem. Always create time when you are just there to listen to your child's ideas, problems and discoveries without talking. Opening up to you will instill self-confidence and they will improve on their esteem issues. When listening to your child, pay particular attention to what they seem to find joy in doing so as to encourage them to get more involved. If she likes ballet, suggest taking them to a ballroom class. Also, manage your tone when you talk to your child while upset. Raising your tone might scare them and make them seclude themselves. When they make a mistake, let your focus be on what they did wrong rather than the wrong doer. Your language should always be positive.

Encourage Exercise

Exercising is known to release feel good hormones that increase your energy levels and improve your moods. You would definitely want your child to enjoy the benefits of exercising. However, they may not be willing to go on the treadmill with you or do some other intensive exercises. In this case, you can engage in more playful activities that they can find fun in. For instance, you can set aside some time every weekend where the whole family can play a game of soccer. Additionally, if they are interested in pets, you can get them a dog and take the dog for a walk together. This will not only ensure that they exercise but will also teach them responsibility of having to take care of the dog.

Teach on Winning and Losing

First of all, you need to give your child the assurance that you love them unconditionally (or no matter what happens); it doesn't matter whether they win or lose since your love for them is unending. You see, children need to be reminded of how much they are valued for who they are and not only when they win. You have to delete from their memory the wrong notion that how well they fare would be the basis of how much their parents would value them. You should always remind your child that it is okay when they fail at something. Failure makes a child feel that they are not good at anything. For instance, if they are a slow learner in class, other children will always be ahead and this will discourage them from going to school. Remind them that a lesson is learnt from losing and the important thing is that they tried and hope should not be lost.

Allow your child to express the emotions that they have at a particular time especially when they are defeated. If they are angry, allow them to vent out their anger rather than speak harshly to them when they are crying. Bottling anger will only lead to depression and in no time, you will be dealing with a depressed child, something that I am sure you would not want to see happen.

Encourage Joining Of Clubs And Organizations

Many school going children are registered in school clubs and organizations. Journalism club, football teams, science club, math club, cheerleaders club and dance club are just a few of the available opportunities in various schools. You should encourage your child to join one of the clubs as they bring about a sense of belonging as the members of the various clubs treat each other as family. In so doing, your child will end up growing as an all-round person because these clubs aim to develop other aspects of your child's life.

Chapter 18: Chores With Children

We decided to start chores with our kids, and give them an allowance to go with it. When we started, we had a set amount they earned each week, but we would take 50 cents away each time they didn't do a job. One daughter decided that she would determine whether she did the job based on how much she lost if she didn't complete it. She would also ask for more money if we asked her to do anything else. So we changed our system.

Assigning chores with children is a great way to teach them the value of work and belonging to a family. In the summer when school is out, we give our children an allowance with the chores and a chore chart with specific jobs each day. During the school year, we take away the chore chart and the allowance, but they are still required to help out around the house when asked. We explain that helping out with the house is part of being a family.Other families handle chores in different ways.

Each family is different, and the children in the family are different as well.It is important to find a system that works with you and your kids, and is easy to manage.No one wants to spend all day harassing their kids to get their work done.And in the real work, a boss wouldn't do this either, they would lose their job. Starting chores is a good way to prepare your children for life.It gives them a sense of purpose and accomplishment, shows the importance of working together as a family, and teaches them that work can be rewarding.Kids are never too young to start with age appropriate jobs.

Getting a Child to Clean their Room

I have had a lot of experience with getting a child to clean their room.Each child is different and what works with one will not work with another.Some children don't need help in this area, this article is written for the ones that do.Rewards and punishments work for some children, but not for others.Some children look at a messy room and have no idea how to begin cleaning it.For kids that are just completely overwhelmed, here are some ideas for helping them.

Break down the job into different areas.For example, have your child pick up all the books in the room.When that is done, have them put all the clothes in a pile.Breaking down the mess into small messes helps make the job more manageable.Make a game out of cleaning.Set a time limit for different items and see what they can clean up the fastest.Write down the times and find out which items was the easiest to clean. Pull everything together in one big pile.Have your child pick out the biggest item from the pile and put that away first.Or find everything that is the color red and put that away.Sometimes just cleaning up in a different way is all it takes to get the job done.

Setting rewards and punishments can work sometimes, but helping your child learn how to manage the mess and get it cleaned timely is the key to success every time.Teaching them how to clean their room saves you from harassing them every day to get it cleaned.And it can give your child a great sense of accomplishment once they are done.

Teaching about the Internet

Kids today have a different perception of the computer and the internet.Children in elementary school are being taught how to use a computer.Some school reports require internet sources.Teaching your children about the internet and setting some rules will help keep them safer. First, help your children understand that seeing something on the internet doesn't make it real.Friends that they meet might not really be children.Help them to understand how the internet makes everyone anonymous.Anyone can create a web site and make their information appear as fact.

Help them set up an email account that you can control.Limit the emails they send out, make sure they are to friends that they know.Set up an email filter so that unwanted email isn't viewable to them.Decide on rules regarding registering for things on web sites, you may not want them doing this. Set a limit on computer time.Experts advise that children have no more than two hours of television, electronic games, or computer use in a day.Monitor their time on the computer to try to keep within these guidelines.

Show them how to search for things they are looking for.There are several great search engines for kids.Some popular search engines that cater to children include www.yahooligans.com and www.ajkids.com.If you allow them to search for information through a search engine, monitor their web browsing to make sure they don't end up where you don't want them. The internet can be a great tool for children, and provided a wealth of information, games, and other fun activities.Monitor their computer time, and watch where they are surfing.Always make sure that your kids are following safety rules when on the internet.

Chapter 19: Security

Of course the internet is not the only place where danger lurks.Kids love to be independent but unfortunately the modern age is fraught with all manner of pitfalls when it comes to venturing out of the house alone, especially for young people.

So how old is old enough to be out of the house alone?This is a question that has been debated at heated length by parents all over the world.The problems encountered are different depending on where you live and the kind of community in which your child has been raised.In major cities it is unusual for children to go to school alone, although there are some school transport arrangements where kids are left at the bus stop and then collected again later.

Mostly, mothers or father schlepp the kids to school on the way to work or get into a car share system.If you do car share remember it is never successful if you are one of those people who constantly want to change your day or even want to dip out altogether when it is your turn – if you do that too many times you will eventually be 'frozen out' and rightly so!

On average, kids start asking to go out alone from around the age of eight or nine although that is not to say this should be permitted. The urge for independence is strong at that age and there will be a dozen plaintive requests: 'Please Mum can I? Georgie does and his mother is okay about it...' This is a grey area and some mothers do allow their kids a long rein when it comes to wandering about town on a Saturday morning (or evening). It very much depends on where you live, although my personal advice would be to say no until your child is at least 14 years old and even then never let him or her go out alone but always ensure a friend tags along.

There is even an element of being tackled by other mothers and fathers on this. You can appreciate that if someone is not allowing their child to do things that yours is permitted to do on a regular basis you might feel your parenting is coming in for some criticism. The point is this is your child: not theirs.

If someone asks you why you will not allow your child to go out in the company of other very young children simply remind them that you make the decisions where your kid is concerned and although you are not criticising, you reserve the right to decide what happens in your child's world. If they are offended: tough. This kind of problem nearly always rears its ugly head around Halloween when 'Trick or Treaters' want to roam around unsupervised. Put your foot down and insist they follow your rules, not someone else's.

Host With The Most

Visiting kids are a joy – yes really they are!From a young age your child will discover the social satisfaction of being able to bring someone home from school or for sleepovers or for meals, parties or just to share a homework table.

There are a number of hurdles that might appear on the kiddie social scene.If your child has a propensity to pick friends from the same cultural background as yours then you are an unusual family!Invariably they choose kids far removed in background, ethnicity and intelligence.That is not to suggest that the other child is inferior to yours – they are simply different.So bear in mind that when your child starts bringing home friends you need to make some enquiries before inviting them to meals and to stay over – some will be Buddhist, others Moslem as well as Christians, vegetarians, vegans or kids with health problems and allergies so they need careful supervision when they eat... the list of possible pitfalls is endless.

The behavioural standards of other children are also likely to be different to that of your own kids.Sometimes you are lucky and get one that is better behaved than yours – unfortunately most of the time you end up with kids that have no table manners, demand junk food, refuse to eat your cooking and want to leave your house looking like a junkyard.Do not put up with appalling behaviour from other peoples' kids. Explain briefly and calmly that that is not allowed in your house – do not shout – and usually it will stop.If it doesn't, just don't issue a repeat invitation and explain to your child the reasons why.

It is always a good idea to get to know another child a little before extending an invitation to stay overnight in your house.Some are eager to stay but then change their minds in the middle of the night and want to go home to mum; some want to stay forever; some never seem to go back to their own house until the day they move into their own apartment!

It is nice to have friends and it can be a joyful thing to have your house full of young faces but remember there are other people to consider when teenagers want to listen to heavy metal at full boom! A little moderation when entertaining teenagers is always a good thing! And remember when your son or daughter wants to invite a friend to tag along on a family holiday that you need to learn a little about them first.

My Kid has Gone Goth

Physical appearance is important to children from the off and by the time they reach their teens they have usually asserted their own authority when it comes to deciding what to wear.

Girls and boys are equally determined to wear what they like and sometimes this can be a problem when what they want to wear is at complete variance to the regulations laid down by the school's uniform guidelines.

In girl-only or boy-only educational establishment the problem is not so bad but there always seems to be a clash of parent /student / teacher views in co-ed schools, probably due to the competition to attract the attentions of this or that person...

Many older children rebel when it comes to wearing the grey pleated skirt and most boys refuse point blank to wear a school cap and who could blame them!However, in many ways the school uniform does help cash-strapped parents to cope with the ever-escalating costs of fashion items. The playground catwalk can be a cruel platform for highlighting who can afford to keep up with the latest fashions and who cannot.

The issue of uniform needs to be approached with some practicality too – skirts and school trousers may of course be worn more than once but school shirts need to be fresh every day so if you cannot afford to buy half a dozen you need to stay on top of the laundry rota!

Teenagers go through all kinds of fad fashions and each stage will be punctuated by some outrageous request to do this or that. Try to stay strong on the issue of tattoos, however. Tattoos seem to have an irresistible lure for kids of a certain age and of course once they are inked onto young skin they are painful and difficult to get rid of and as the child gets older – and hopefully more sensible – the tattoo becomes more embarrassing. Try to persuade your kid that a temporary tattoo is just as cool and not as disfiguring.

Piercings, though just as unsightly, are actually not as disastrous as tattooing because holes will heal over usually. Your 16-year-old may beg and plead for a belly clip and you may eventually cave in but before you do try persuading her to try a hinged variety that does not involve an actual piercing.

Chapter 20: Helping Your Child Overcome Fear And Become Courageous

As a parent, your most important goals should be to empower your child, and equip him or her with the necessary courage and strength needed to handle all the obstacles life throws his or her way.

Being strong, brave, and courageous are important elements required to grow a positive mindset. When you are positive and believe in becoming better, you perceive every obstacle as an adventure and achieve the courage required to boldly face that obstacle. This attitude helps you move past each struggle easily and live the kind of life you desire. By helping your child create a growth mindset, you will impart these qualities on him or her.

How To Help Your Child Overcome Fear And Become Courageous

Let us look at the techniques you can use to arm your child with the ability to soar high in his or her life and gracefully handle each failure.

Do not protect your child against failure: Being the parent might make you feel as if you have to shield your child from pain and harm; which is why you might not let your child participate in contests, so that the child does not face any rejection or failure.

Although you have the best intention, you are making your child be vulnerable to failure. According to Madeline Levine, author of "The Price of Privilege: How Parental Pressure and Material Advantage Are Creating a Generation of Disconnected and Unhappy Kids" a popular book on parenting, most parents perceive failure as a painful experience for children rather than seeing it as an opportunity to shape a child's strength and confidence. This is why most parents do their best to keep children away from events that can trigger rejection. Madeline Levine believes it is not healthy to do this and parents need to let children face rejections, obstacles, and failures.

Why You Should Let Your Children Experience Rejection

Letting your child experience denial, defeat, and various failures is important because it develops in your child key components such as emotional resilience, capability to collaborate, creative thinking, and coping skills he or she needs to succeed in different life ventures.

When your child faces any type of rejection, you should be by your child's side telling him or her that life does not end at this rejection and this defeat is there to help him or her become better; this is the kind of support your child needs.

Help your children look for probable solutions to a problem: Act as your child's guide and not his or her savior. Let's face it; you won't be there every time your child faces an obstacle. Therefore, you must teach your child how to tackle obstacles rather than escaping them.

One good tactic for doing that is to guide your child to think of probable solutions to any problem. Vickie Falcone, bestselling author of "You Can't Make Me: **How to Parent with More Connecting and Less Correcting**" suggests that parents should help children brainstorm for ideas to tackle various difficult situations.

If your child comes crying to you with a problem, don't start solving the problem; instead, ask your child to first think of ways to resolve the situation on their own before you offer your input. Doing this helps your child become independent and understand that he or she needs to face problems head on, and boldly face all the obstacles life will present.

Empathize with your child's disappointment: While it is important you let your child face different obstacles so he or she can feel the pain and become stronger, it is also essential to empathize with your child's pain and let him or her know that you're there. When you find your child sulking, blue, depressed, or sad, talk to your child. Let the child pour his or her heart out to you. You can then share similar experiences with your child to show him or her that he or she is not alone in this; you, along with many other people have faced similar problems in life. This strengthens your child and helps him or her cope with the problem.

Teach your child different self-calming tactics: Teach your child different self-calming techniques. When you do, your child learns how to soothe him, or herself when a problem arises. This helps your child successfully cope with rejection, struggle, and life failures. In her book: "Dealing with Disappointment: **Helping Kids Cope when Things Don't Go Their Way**," Elizabeth Cary discusses six amazing types of self-soothing techniques for children.

Self-Soothing Techniques for Children

Let us look at these strategies.

Physical Tactics

Physical tactics, such as physical activity and breathing techniques are excellent at helping children channel aggression in a positive manner after facing a failure. Physical exercise helps children get rid of negative energy, and breathing calms your child. Teach your child to take deep breaths and blow away feathers or candles whenever he or she feels stressed.

Verbal/Auditory Strategies

Verbal strategies help your child handle stress related to different problems by discussing problems with a supportive person, performing positive self-talk, and listening to calming or inspiring music.

Endear yourself to your child until you become your child's supportive person so that your child does not fall prey to placing his or her faith in the wrong person. Positive self-talk refers to giving healthy suggestions to yourself. Teach your child this tactic offering your child a difficult situation and developing positive suggestions for it.

For instance, say this to your child; "If you face a big obstacle, don't tell yourself that you cannot battle it." Instead, tell yourself you will successfully resolve it and resolving it will make you better. This type of talk gives you hope and motivates you to face your problems with valor. As for the music technique, find out what type of music inspires and calms your child and make sure to play it whenever your child feels tensed.

Visual Tactics

Visual tactics include reading motivational stories and playing games such as 'I spy.' that help distract your child from feelings of rejection and disappointments,

Creative techniques to help your child bravely face problems include asking your child to draw his or her feelings, or create something, such as building play dough sculptures, using blocks, or cooking something; these tactics help release the restless energy mounting inside.

Self-Calming Methods

To make your child feel loved, give your child a warm hug so he or she can feel relaxed. Alternatively, when you child is feeling stressed ask him or her to take a relaxing, warm bath because baths are helpful at eliminating irritating feelings.

Humor Tactics

Another powerful tactic guaranteed to help your child calm down is humor. When your child is feeling sad or stressed, he or she could read humorous books, or watch entertaining videos. You could also try crack a joke or two to cheer up your child. This technique often proves successful; therefore, do teach it to your child.

Make efforts to teach your child one tactic at a time, so that he or she learns how to soothe worries independently, and become confident individuals.

Teach your child to face fear: In addition to doing the above, you also have to teach your child how to face fear so that your child becomes bold enough to take risks in life and have new experiences.

For that, you need to be patient with your child. Never coax your child into facing his or her fears; instead, take things slow. Begin with teaching your child the significance of doing this: it will make your child fearless.

You can bring in your child's favorite superhero into this discussion and inspire your child to be like the superhero. Tell your child that a superhero is amazing, and a hero because he or she faced his or her fears and did not stop when things became increasingly difficult. If your child wants to follow in his or her superheroes' example, your child then needs to become a hero and face his or her fear. Encourage your child to be brave and bold and appreciate your child when he or she makes a very tiny move towards facing his or her fears.

Teach your child to be grateful for what he or she has: Work to teach your child to be grateful for what he or she has. Gratitude helps your child become aware of life's many blessings. When your child gains this realization, he or she stops fretting over what he or she has lost. This goes on to help the child overcome the pain of rejection.

Therefore, ask your child to list everything he or she is grateful for, and then show your child examples of other children who do not have as much. This comparison will help your child better understand how truly blessed he or she is, which will help your child stop crying over small losses and failures.

Teach your child to take each day as it comes: To ensure your child never backs out of a challenge, and faces every struggle boldly, teach your child to take life as an adventure, and take each moment as it comes. Tell your child that nobody has the power to predict the future, but when you take each day as it comes, you become powerful enough to battle every challenge as it arises. Every day is going to bring with it new challenges and opportunities; your child needs to accept this. Once he or she realizes that, he or she starts feeling less scared of facing challenges.

Practice these strategies to infuse in your child the strength, valor, and patience to handle failures gracefully, and tackle obstacles fearlessly like a pro.

Chapter 21: No Two Kids Are The Same

Are you sitting down?Good.Now, swallow your drink.Okay, I have six kids.Yeah, you read that right.My basketball team has a bench.There are a lot of things that having a larger than average family has taught me but the most important is probably the fact that no two children are the same.

Even when they have the same parents, grow up in the same house, and go to the same church and school their whole lives.Each child has his or her own interests, mannerisms and personality quirks.

That means there is no one 'method' of parenting.I have six kids so I have six methods of parenting.Yes, my rules and basic expectations for them are all the same, but I apply them differently.

For one, cleaning the room might mean dusting every nook and cranny, for another, it just means getting the clothes put away.For one, a punishment is giving her extra work.Another needs to have something taken away.Different approaches get different responses from different kids but it is all geared to the same end of raising them to be the best people that they can be.

It will take some time for you to learn your children's differences.This will come just from playing with them, watching how they interact with others and just seeing how they respond to different situations.

A byproduct of this is that you will only rarely be able to accommodate them all at the same time.Different kids will want to go to the park, while others to the beach, while others would prefer to just stay home and read.

Quite simply, trying to make them all happy at the same time all the time will drive you bonkers.The best thing that you can do in those situations is to set your expectations, and promise those protesting that they will get to pick next time.

Don't take this to mean that you shouldn't seek out advice or even spend some time reading those parenting books to get some ideas of how to handle certain situations.

 Just don't expect to apply the exact same methods to even just one kid.Take the principles you learn and find ways to apply them to your own situation.Trying to use them as a cookie-cutter will just result in a very hot mess.Insert chapter here...

Chapter 22: Strategic Listening

In order to make any relationships work, mutual understanding is a must. That can only be accomplished by listening intently to what the other person is trying to communicate, and vice versa. We may have assumptions about what the other person is trying to say, but we really do not know what exactly they're trying to communicate unless we first listen intently and then clarify any doubts we have about what we're hearing.

Exercising what I'd call strategic listening – the act of first listening intently without interruptions, then clarifying any doubts we have about what we're hearing, before we respond – helps us to better manage our child's behavior and build mutual understanding.

How To Exercise Strategic Listening

The following is a step-by-step guide towards exercising strategic listening:

Firstly, if possible, remove your kid from the site / object that triggered the tantrum — There will always be some form of stimulus that makes your child's emotional state go haywire. It could be losing something important, not getting what they want, feeling uncomfortable, and the list goes on. Once you've identified the cause, gently bring them out of the place, so that you can proceed to step 2.

Allow them to calm down — Nothing good ever comes from fighting fire with fire. Recall the three elements you have read in Chapter 2. After you've taken the child to some place to take a breather, allow them space to calm down. Some children recover quickly while others take a slightly longer time. The key is to allow them to calm down.

Listen intently — Just that, listen to whatever the child is telling you. Give them your fullest attention. The only thing we can do at this stage is to hang on to every word they're saying, nod to acknowledge we're listening, and not jump to conclusions or try to interrupt them. It's not that we cannot speak up as parents, but we should first seek to understand where they're coming from, so that we can ask better questions and craft a better response.

Ask questions – Whatever doubts we have, now it's the time to clarify them with our children. "And why do you feel sad about not being able to join the school excursion?", "Do you fear missing out on the fun?" By asking questions, we help ourselves better understand why our children feel the way they do, and why they behaved the way they do.

You'd be surprised at how far strategic listening can go and how it can make your life a whole lot easier. Children seek to feel heard, understood, and that they're safe.

Most of all, they want to feel that you care.

I wouldn't say that I'm a perfect mother, but I have since come a long way.

Parenthood is indeed full of challenges. But we are not entirely helpless. By following the above advice, I am highly-confident that you too will reap the joys of parenthood like I did!

Chapter 23: Transition Strategies

Depending on the age of the child during the divorce, there are some strategies that you can often use to help make the transition easier. For instance, reading books with your child can be helpful for younger aged children.

You've probably heard of psychologists who use puppets or stories to allow a child to express their feelings after they have been abused. This is a similar thought process for parents. Allow characters in books to become outlets for the child to express and understand their own feelings.

If you can find books on divorce that are written for children which allow them to see characters experiencing the same kind of feelings they are, the child won't feel nearly as alone. You can read the stories aloud or allow the child to read them to you if they are able.

Often, kids won't have any idea that these books are meant to help them through the divorce.They'll think that they're just entertainment like any other book, but it will allow you to get some important messages across to the child. It gives you a chance to communicate through the characters and make important points about the current family situation.

Aside from the content in the book, children feel closer and more attached when you read and tell stories together.After reading, you can also open up the lines of communication by asking them questions about what they thought of the book.

Often, children will speak specifically about the characters and not about themselves.However, their internal feelings about the characters and their situations will give you a direct window into what's going on inside of them.

Ask some open-ended questions so that you give the child a reason to talk.You can ask therapists or even your local librarian if they have any recommendations for books of this nature that will help a child through divorce.In addition, you can read some fiction classics that also give really good information about dealing with stress, adversity or loss.

As mentioned before, children will often show their emotions when they are playing.This is particularly good for young children because they can express their feelings quite easily through the act of playing.Often, parents can understand what's going on with the child just by watching them play or playing with them.

For instance, you might want to sit down with a young girl and play with Barbies.You could use G.I. Joe or action figures for a young boy.Allow them to act out different scenes and really listen to what they're saying and how they are reacting to situations.

Don't impose your feelings on the child, however.Only join into play if the child asks you to.Don't direct them while they're playing, just let them enjoy it.If they think you're watching them or trying to get information from them, they'll start to feel uncomfortable.You can use all kinds of things during playtime from chalk to sand to boardgames to puppets.

Communicating

Another important part of getting to the heart of the matter when it comes to walking your child through divorce is talking with them and communicating.However, it can be very difficult for some parents to have the right words to use when it comes to explaining a divorce.These sensitive issues can be extremely hard to explain to adults, much less children.

Here are some things that you can say when you are explaining the situation to your child:

•You are not alone.You have lots of friends and family who love you and will be there to support you. You have two parents who will always love you and be there for you.

- A separation is when parents decide that they need to live apart from each other for a while and think about whether they want to stay married. No matter what we decide, we will always be your parents and be there for you.
- I understand that the separation is a very hard thing to talk about. It might be difficult for you to tell people that your mom and dad are no longer living together.
- Lots of kids want their parents to stay together, and that's normal. But, sometimes things are better for the whole family when parents decide to separate. It's normal for you to be upset, and it's okay for you to talk about it with me.
- It's normal for kids to feel caught in the middle during a separation, but we don't want you to feel that way. We both love you, and our divorce has nothing to do with you or anything that you did wrong.

For the non-custodial parent, it's very important to explain to the child that you leaving the house is not connected to your love for them. You have to explain that the only reason you're leaving is because you aren't getting along. The child needs to understand that you love them as much as you always have, and that you always will.

Explain to the child that a divorce is simply when two people decide that they don't want to be married to each other anymore because they can't be happy that way. Explain that you just decided to stop being husband and wife, but you will always be their parents. Never say, "I didn't want the divorce. Your mother did," or anything like that. It sets the child up for anger at one parent, and that is not fair to anyone.

You have to make sure that your children know that you'll always be their mother and father, and they will still have a family even after a divorce.

Telling the child that children can never cause a divorce and that they can never keep a mother and father together is important.

You should also explain, in age-appropriate terms, that during the divorce at least one parent has to go talk to the judge in a court room to figure out the rules for the divorce.Then a lawyer and a judge will draw up the right paperwork to explain how caring for the children and visitation with the children will work.

Chapter 24: Summary And Tips

The following is a summary of all the tips and tantrum proofing techniques mentioned and discussed in this book. It serves as an easy reference to help you remember. If you need to, take time to review the contents of the book.

Preventing Tantrums

- Toddler proof the entire home
- Establish a routine for your kids
- Give your kids (and yourself) plenty of time and opportunity to let off steam
- Keep frustration levels to a minimum for you and your kid
- Give them a choice – don't just tell them to stop (remember the options you will give)
- Distractions work like magic – have some ready

- Remember that your child is the one with the problem – don't jump into the stress bandwagon

Measure the Tantrum Level
- Classify if the tantrum is only a minor episode
- Know what to do in case of a major tantrum

Dealing with Minor Tantrums
- Ignore the tantrum for a certain period of time
- Use calming techniques on yourself
- After the ignore time is over see if your child can be jollied
- Remember that you can always pick up your child away from public view (cuts down your own embarrassment)

Dealing with Major Tantrums
- Weather the storm
- Remember to speak calmly
- Take time outs

- Make eye contact when speaking to your child
- Calm yourself first before dealing with your child

A Few Useful Reminders

Kids Usually Outgrow Tantrum City

Remember that for most kids, tantrums only last during the early development stage. They eventually grow out of it. As their vocabulary and communication skills develop, they learn to communicate and express their feelings much better. Thus in the end they no longer find the need to have tantrums.

Remember that Laughter and Overall Goofiness Works

Humor can be a big cure for these tricky situations with toddlers. Silly songs, jokes, and anything that can induce laughter for your child can help diffuse a tense situation. Sometimes all you need to do is to give them a hug, some comfort, and a timely tickle. If you can lighten up the mood you can set things straight.

Always remember that harsh discipline will only feed the tantrum and make it worse. Punishments don't work on young children. Positive reinforcement is actually more effective.

Even Little Children Have Feelings

Your toddler also has feelings and a tantrum is just one way (albeit sometimes a really extreme way) of expressing their feelings. If they feel that they are understood then they will slowly lose the need to use tantrums. Let them know that you understand that they are mad or even sad. Acknowledge and respect those feelings. Even better, teach them to express their feelings in words.

Bracing Yourself for a Tidal Wave of Emotions

Observe your children. Their emotions can sometimes rise and fall like that of waves of the sea. If they are tired or stressed then they escalate until they eventually break into a tantrum. Take note of the stressors and any situation that has caused a tantrum. Try to avoid bringing your child into such situations.

However, some situations and stressors are necessary – such as potty training or their first day in the nursery. There's just no way to avoid them. That means you just have to brace yourself and be prepared to console, show sympathy, and practice some patience.

Toddlers Learn by Observation

It's kind of surprising for some that toddlers can learn quite a lot at such a young age. Most of the time they emulate what their parents are doing. If they see you happy, relaxed, and calm always (or most of the time) then they will emulate that. They will also tend to be jolly and calm.

Chapter 25: Education Woes

Because of the social times that we live in, single parenting is widely accepted and it has to be, because unfortunately the number of single parent households is approaching the same as households with two parents, society is producing a generation of children and teens with emotional issues that can impair them well after their formative years and into their adult existence.

Parenting is by far the hardest job anybody can sign on to complete, and with parenting, the job is never complete. You are never able to cross the finish line and say I am done – parenting is a lifelong commitment of selflessness and should only be entered into with extreme caution and understanding child rearing.

There have been a number of studies that have shown the positives of kids raised in households where there are two parents. And although there are definitely cases where kids have demonstrated behavioral, emotional or other types of issues, those characteristics are more widely seen in kids and teens of single parents.The stability alone of a duo parenting household creates an environment that gives children and teens and a feeling of security.The majority of kids raised in single parent households suffer from feelings of insecurity and abandonment.These feelings result in an inability to have solid relationships in the future.

But aside from the emotional effects that will manifest themselves, kids suffer academically.Of course many kids do well regardless of their situation, but statistically, students of broken homes or that are being raised in a single parent environment do not perform nearly as well as those in a two parent environment.The high majority of students that were unsuccessful in the classroom are reportedly from a single parent home environment.Much of this stems from the parent not being available to assist the child with homework, enforce good study habits and establish rules for their child.A large part of a child or teen's inability to do well in school is from the inability to handle the emotional stress that come with being raised in a single home or a product of a divorced home.

Many of the students are performing academically well below their peers and well below their ability.There is a lack of interest and desire that has been found in children of single parent homes.Children of divorced parents and or being raised by a single parent are two times more likely to drop out of high school than their peers who are living with both parents.That statistic should raise eyebrows in concern.We are producing a generation of illiterate people as a result of divorce and choice to single parent.

It is difficult to sit idly by and not want to jump with frustration at the ever growing epidemic of single parenthood. Can we change this? Perhaps if people would begin to put a face to the statistic and recognize that these are lost lives, children and teens who are being robbed of so much either through divorce or the choice to be a single parent.

Chapter 26: When Royals Produce Peasants

Sometimes the best of parents have children that do not 'turn out right.'Sometimes bad parents produce extraordinary offspring.Life is not always fair.You can try and play God, attempting to control your child's every move, every friend, every thought.How do you think that will work for you?In doing so you will either produce a child who has not a single ability to think for himself or a child that will give a rebel yell, say you are number one with the wrong finger and make you wish you had been sterile from the get go.Yet if you allow your children the opportunity of free will, they will freely exercise it.This reality can seem like there is no way to win.

I grew up knowing the family of a pastor.The family had three children, two of whom turned out to be respectable: both as children, and later as adults.Yet the eldest proved to be anything but a good citizen.Friends opened up their homes to him, hoping they might lend a hand in guiding him back from the darkness of addiction.Some of them lived far enough away that utilizing their geographic location constituted a new start.Yet the young man could not stop making poor choices in spite of the fact that an entire village had done all that it could to save him from his own worst enemy: himself.

There in, lies the quandary.If we try to play God and force our will on our children, we will fail them.Ultimately, they will make their own choices: whether we like it, or not.Our job as parents is not to make their choices for them, but rather, to teach them how each and every choice (every action) has an equal and opposite reaction.Some of those reactions are good.Some of those reactions are bad.

The reality we have to accept is that some people only learn by touching the stove.Some people never learn.Maybe your child is one of them.There is always that child whose parent has to watch her like a hawk in order to keep her from burning herself.The stress level is elevated.Energy is overspent.Yet all the parent has to do is let the child burn herself and the lesson might be learned.Or maybe that child will not learn her lesson.Overprotection, however, will not facilitate the process.Either the child will learn, or the child will not.Overprotection will only make the parents' elevated stress levels- due to a struggling child- exponentially increase.

Yet that is the quandary, is it not?How can a loving parent allow any harm to come to their child?Not protecting our child goes against every fabric of our being.We are like the doctors who, because of the Hippocratic Oath, literally prolong the suffering of the patient in the name of preserving life.Sometimes love is not very nice.Sometimes love means forcing them into rehab, holding them back a year in school, or letting her heart get broken.Such things do feel as if they hurt us, as parents, more than they hurt them, as children.

Yet our children need permission to fail.My newest joy in life is golf.Probably the greatest lesson golf teaches us is that one failure does not ruin your opportunity to succeed.One bad shot on a hole does not preclude the player from success.What it does do is make success a greater challenge.A bad shot makes the next shot further than it needs to be, more complex than it has to be or carry a higher degree of difficulty than other wise would have been necessary.But one bad shot does not prevent success.

Life is no different.Our image of our mothers is not always catching us when we fall, but kissing our boo-boos.Skinned knees were often the results of failure: failure to balance a bike; failure to avoid tripping; failure to land correctly after jumping over the fence.Good moms did not keep us from running or jumping or riding our bikes.Nor did they discourage us from doing those things again after they dried our tears and cleaned our wounds.We learned from those failures because our mother's encouraged us to run and jump and ride again.Your children, likewise, have to learn to get back up on that 'horse-' what ever that horse may be.

What our parents taught us (or should have taught us) was that the reward outweighed the risk.The consequences of failure teach us to succeed.For the vast majority of us, skinned knees did not inhibit bike riding- skinned knees virtually guaranteed it.That is all you can do as a parent.Taking away the consequences will only guarantee an adult child who has no ability to assess risk.Inflating the consequences will simply stifle your child's emotional growth.

All we can do is teach our children the proper rewards and consequences for each action they might choose to take.There are three ways in which we can do this.Our modern society is the first culture absent of true rights of passage.We might say that driving or graduating from high school are rights of passage, but how does that compare with the tribal right of a young man succeeding on his first solo hunt?While I do not believe that every teenage boy needs to head off into the forest alone, the point is that the ancient rites had a way of proving to the boy or girl that he or she had passed through that proverbial portal into adulthood.What that looks like for your child might be different than what it looks like for my child.However, what that right of passage should not look like is the over-consumption of drugs or alcohol, or sexual promiscuity.

Long before we can lay before our children a right of passage, we must teach them to be relentless life warriors.We need to have tenacious children.I once heard a speaker whose profound solution to those times in life when you 'fall down' was simply to, 'get up.' That is the tenacity we need to teach our children. You can try all you want to teach your children that failure is not an option and they will simply try to cover up their mistakes--- just like you do. Or you can teach them to fail their way to success and they will live relentlessly.

Finally, as we accept the fact that even the most successful parents can have 'failed' children, we need to take a good hard look in the mirror. We, as humans, can justify almost anything we do. I can say I am good man and overlook the faults and weaknesses I personally need to overcome. I can talk sweet to people outside my family and yell at the ones inside my nuclear unit. I can give strangers warm hugs while I give my children cold shoulders. Yet if what I want from my children is for them to become better persons in their own right, I must lead the way.

Chapter 27: How And When To Introduce A New Relationship

When you first get divorced, a new relationship will likely be the last thing on your mind. But as you move forward in your healing journey, you may find that you're ready to give it another go. Introducing a new relationship to your children can be a challenging venture, and the key is to take it slow and have low expectations in the beginning.

Protecting Yourself

The world of dating can be a scary one, and if you've been out of the game for awhile, you may have forgotten the basic rules. Emotionally balanced children have emotionally balanced parents, so you'll need to keep yourself safe as you navigate the challenging waters of dating. Remember these key rules:

Meet a new person only in a public location, and avoid being alone with someone until you've interacted with them several times. It can even be a good idea to search him or her on the Internet to make sure they are who they say they are. After all, your children's safety is paramount when it comes to a new relationship.

Avoid rebounding. If you're still crying over your ex or jealous of his or her love life, you're not yet ready to date yet.

Don't rush into a new relationship. The right person will be willing to take it slow.

Date around before you settle on a new relationship. Your post-divorce time is a great opportunity to explore your own needs. Rushing into the arms of a new person may lead to the exact same problems you experienced in your marriage.

Putting Kids First

When you were younger and single, you had the luxury of playing the field, perhaps even dating people who weren't quite right for you. However, now that you're a single parent, your kids come first – no ifs, ands, or buts. This means that anyone you date needs to know that you have kids and be willing to play a loving role in their lives. Some keys for putting your kids first are:

DO choose people who, at the very least, like or enjoy being around kids, or maybe even have kids of their own.

DO place the needs of your children before the needs of your new romance. For example, don't ditch your kids for a date or date someone who is unfriendly toward your children.

DO keep romantic behavior away from your kids. Children are made uncomfortable by kissing and touchy-feely behavior, and this can trigger their sadness about their parents' divorce.

DO start slowly. Introduce your child to a new romance, then gradually increase the time your partner spends with your child over several months. It's best to do the introductions in a fun setting, such as a party or when your child is already happy and in a good mood. It's best to talk to your child about the romantic interest prior to doing any introductions.

DON'T leave a new romantic interest alone with your children; they must earn your complete trust first.

DON'T introduce someone to your children until you're absolutely certain the relationship will be a long-term one. Kids suffer when adults suddenly come into their lives and leave a short time later.

DON'T let your partner discipline your kids. His or her role is to be a fun and trustworthy adult, not a second parent.

DON'T get into fights with or insult your ex's romantic interests.

DON'T allow your romantic interest to make negative comments about your child or about your ex to your child.

The Rules of Dating

Children frequently resent their parents' new romantic partners. They can worry that they are being replaced or that their other parent will disappear when their parents start dating. Consequently, you'll need to have low expectations in the beginning. Some key points to remember are:

Your child doesn't have to like the person you're dating, and you shouldn't force him to. Instead, he simply has to behave in a respectful way – the same way he would treat a teacher or family member.

If you break up with a romantic partner, be prepared for your child to be sad. It's ideal to choose partners who will continue their relationship with your child even if your romantic relationship ends.

Ask your child how he feels about your new romantic partner, and don't get angry if he expresses negativity.

Explicitly tell your child that no new romance can replace him or his other parent.

Conclusion

Divorce is bitter. It's that division of a family that brings with it all the negativity that children can experience in their lives. Two people that they love no longer love each other. When you become a single dad and you remember that kids need to feel security and love, all the rest follows as a natural progression.

Don't expect to be perfect. No parent is and that includes parents who stay together. You are no less of a parent and although you may be looking for advice and encouragement, you will find that all things happen the way that they should if you approach them with an open heart and a positive and caring attitude.

When you do, your children will amaze you with their strength and will help you through troubled times, just as they expect you to be there for them when their little lives throw dilemmas their way. With positivity and lack of bitterness, you can rebuild their lives with you and always depend upon the family unit as being strong, even if there is only one parent. The love you share with your kids is repaid a thousand times during the course of a lifetime. Your smiles matter more than your inadequacies. Your laughter counts more than your anger at life and your positive love toward your kids counts more than all the leftover bitterness of things that have passed.

www.ingramcontent.com/pod-product-compliance
Lightning Source LLC
Chambersburg PA
CBHW072012070526
44583CB00015B/1452